# NEVER WORK AGAIN

## Work Less, Earn More & Live Your Freedom

## Erlend Bakke

PRAISE FOR

# NEVER WORK AGAIN:

"If you're serious about becoming an entrepreneur then *Never Work Again* will help you find your passion - the passion that will be the key to your success."

**Mike Michalowicz -**
Author of *The Toilet Paper Entrepreneur*

"Erlend's book makes building a virtual business simple. Great practical steps, whether you plan to run your business from home or from the beach! If you liked *The 4-Hour Workweek* you'll love *Never Work Again*."

**Mark Anastasi -**
Author of New York Times bestseller
*The Laptop Millionaire*

"Erlend provides inspiration and gives practical advice to make sure you will never work again. Well done, Mr. Outsource!"

**Carl Gould -**
Author of *The 7 Stages of Small Business Success*

"Success in life is about taking action and *Never Work Again* shows you exactly how to do that to build your own virtual outsourced business and begin living the lifestyle of your dreams."

**Steven Essa**
International speaker and webinar expert

"Never Work Again will help you get great results and get them fast. Use it to help you get ahead of the game."

**Cindy Rold -**
Tony Robbins Platinum and Master Elite Coach

"Many people write books based on what they hope will work. This book is written by an entrepreneur who walks his talk and has actually achieved a success that most other authors can only dream about. Reading this book will give you an excellent insight into how he achieved this success and will also provide a number of practical tools and exercises that you can use in your own business. Recommended."

**Rick Salmon,**
Entrepreneur Coach and Seminar Leader

"I've read numerous books promising wealth and less work, and they are all basically the same. This one is different. Motivational, inspirational, practical, and very, very helpful. Highly recommended for anyone wanting to start a business, already struggling with a business, or for those who have achieved some level of success... you will find something new in this one!"

**Danielle Marie,**
Amazon.com Reviewer

"I got many insights while reading this book and I am now starting to implement some of the ideas. I will definitely recommend this book to anyone interested in getting more free time to do what they love."

**Oyvind Dahl,**
Amazon.com Reviewer

"Erlend helps you explore yourself and what you really want from life and your "job." He's learned himself that it's about far more than just making money, or having material possessions. It's about real peace within yourself. Erlend is an inspiration and I highly recommend his book and his philosophy to any entrepreneur or anyone interested in achieving what they truly want out of life."

**Rick Hart,**
Amazon.com Reviewer

"If you are looking for some insight into a get rich quick scheme this is not for you – those books and programs are bogus and don't work. This book shows you how to make money – period. No gimmicks, just a series of great ideas and stories."

**Todd Thiede,**
Amazon.com Reviewer

"The book is on-point and packed with helpful tips and ideas. I would suggest that this book be dipped into constantly for the budding entrepreneur; especially if you are serious about your dream. The authors' writing style is uplifting and inspiring, and this makes for an encouraging read. I would definitely recommend this book as a gift to inspire others, or to keep on your own digital bookshelf as encouragement for yourself!"

**Piaras O Cionnaioth,**
Amazon.com Reviewer

"An innovative and stimulating business guide book that has left me feeling ready to move out of the exhausting and bland rut I've been stuck in for so long. There are ideas on every page, and thoughts on changing habits (many of which I admit I just never thought about) and I find myself thinking of money and financial opportunities in a new way."

**Beryl Stafford,**
Amazon.com Reviewer

"I feel that this book is a real step towards a very important change in how we all should be doing business. It is representing a real heart, a way of sharing, giving back to all of the people that are mentioned in his book. But also leading the way for all of us to follow. Erlend is one of very few people that I know that are 'walking the walk' instead of just talking. Erlend has understood the principles of sharing, being a caring person, and implementing love as a key factor in how to do business."

**Tor Arne Håve,**
Social Entrepreneur

# Table of Contents

# Index of Exercises

# About the Author

**Erlend Bakke** is a Norwegian serial entrepreneur, speaker, and #1 international bestselling author born in 1981 in London, UK. He currently owns the following three companies: *Mr. Outsource, 3sixty*, and *3sixtyfactory*. Erlend speaks on the topics of entrepreneurship with focus on how to automate and outsource your business to avoid the trap of becoming a business prisoner. He spends most of his  time between London, Oslo, and Davao City in the Philippines, but is available to speak at venues all over the world depending on availability.

Erlend trains entrepreneurs in how to start, run, and own freedom businesses through his seminar `The Freedom Bootcamp` (www.thefreedombootcamp.com), the membership website www.worklessearnmore.tv, and his weekly business podcast `Hardcore MBA Podcast` (www.hardcoremba.com). In 2013 he first published the book **Never Work Again** that went on to become an *#1 International Bestseller*. The book is focused on applying freedom to your life as well as your business by cutting the crap and getting real about your true needs and desires.

**You can email Erlend at: erlend@mroutsource.com**

# Foreword

The first edition of *Never Work Again* was published on 1 September 2013 from a deckchair in Bulgaria overlooking the Black Sea, after a whirlwind two months of activity between myself and the people who helped me to plan and execute the book. My aim was to create a resource that could help others to take advantage of the knowledge and experiences that I have built up over the course of several years of building successful businesses. That's been a long journey for me, and at times a really challenging one as well – I wanted to share the details of some of the lessons I had learned, in the hope that budding entrepreneurs could skip straight past the mistake-making, trial-and-error part and go straight to experiencing the joy of living a more free and happy life.

What has happened since has exceeded my wildest expectations. At the time of writing, *Never Work Again* is now in the hands of over 115,000 people around the world – many of them who have long wanted to start their own business, but have never yet found the motivation, the time, or the inspiration to take that vital first step. Some of them have told me that they feel like they have that motivation now, and those are the kind of emails I live to receive. At the time of writing, the book has over 200 five star reviews on Amazon, and many of the reviewers tell similar stories of feeling inspired to begin a new chapter in their life after reading. It's hit #1 spots on Amazon bestseller lists in four different countries, and my webinars and real-life seminars are overflowing with people who tell me they want to know more.

At the same time, reviewers, friends, and followers who have been in contact since publication have very helpfully pointed to parts of the book that could do with a little improvement. Things that were not fully explained, connections that were not convincingly made, lessons that had been left out. Now, over a year later, and in the spirit of crowdsourcing and collaboration that the internet era nurtures, I think it's time to re-evaluate my words and tighten the book up a little. I think of *Never Work Again* as a fluid document, rather than something that is set in stone – and when people give feedback, I intend to take it on board and strengthen the book wherever possible. This is just one of the revolutionary new possibilities for the publishing industry that the internet has opened up.

Things are now a little clearer, diagrams are explained in more detail, there are more examples of how to put things into practice, and some of the more rambling and unconnected sections have been pruned – when you're as excited about living this life as I am at the moment, it can sometimes be hard to stop talking about it, but "brevity is the soul of wit" as Shakespeare once said, and I have tried to keep things simple and to the point, to make the book as accessible as possible to people from all walks of life.

To stay true to that promise, I will end my foreword here. It remains merely to wish you the best of luck in starting your business and taking it to the next level, and I hope that *Never Work Again* will be able to help you along every step of the way. Enjoy.

**Erlend Bakke**

# Free Book Guide

This book is dedicated to those that seek to have their own freedom lifestyle business.

- Detailed entrepreneurship video training

- Downloadable bonus .mp3 audio

- PDF resources and guides

To get the free book guide and get started on your own successful lifestyle business, please visit:

**YouWillNeverWorkAgain.com/bonus**

(Note: all of the resources referenced throughout this book are stored at this one location.)

# CHAPTER 1

# Introduction: No Pain, No Gain?

*"Once we know that life is difficult –
once we truly understand and accept it –
then life is no longer difficult."*

~**M. Scott Peck,**
"The Road Less Traveled"

## Freedom

*Malibu, California, November 2012* – I gaze over the Pacific from the deck of one of Malibu's favorite seafood restaurants, *Geoffrey's*. The restaurant has been frequented by billionaires, celebrities, and entrepreneurs for years on end. It's a beautiful place, and I should feel like I belong here – I've sat in beautiful places just like this all over the world. But for some reason it feels different this time. Suddenly, I realize something that should have seemed obvious – I was eating alone, and I was bored. Of course, I knew I was by myself when I went into the restaurant, but it was only at this moment that it really struck me that I was lonely. And what I realized at that moment was that ever since I had started my first company in 2007, what I had been pursuing deep down was freedom; but now that I had achieved my goal by making more time and more money for myself, I didn't know what I was meant to do with it all. I realized that I genuinely had no idea what freedom really meant to me.

## Knockout

*Baker Street, London, February 2007* – I see my boss coming over to my desk and I know something is up. "Let's go to the pub," he says, and I immediately know that I'm either getting promoted or fired, and I think *oh boy*. Working in brand consulting was my dream job, it was what I'd prepared myself for doing at university. The second thought that goes through my head is that if I get fired I have no idea how I'm going to pay the rent next month and my girlfriend at the time was not going to like that very much.

We sit down with a pint each, and he looks me in the eyes and I already know which way this is going. "Erlend, this isn't really working out. I don't think you're really made for this kind of work – you should either go and be an egghead at a university, or you should be an entrepreneur. In all honesty, I think you were born for the second of those options." I just look at him. I've never been fired before, and I don't really know what to say. I thank him for the opportunity and leave feeling like I've just gone ten rounds with Mike Tyson. A bottle of whiskey later, I wake up and I know that I need to do some real soul searching. I first started making my own money when I was aged 14, so I guess that maybe I was born to be an entrepreneur – but how do you start becoming an *actual* entrepreneur? I'd never really thought of 'entrepreneur' as a viable career path – it's not exactly something the careers advisor tells you about in school. What do you actually *do* to be be an entrepreneur? Well, I was about to find out.

## Humble Beginnings

*Uxbridge, London, Four Days Later* – James opens the door to our new office. There's a heap of garbage in the middle of the floor, and a wall missing. It's cold, damp and dirty – this old building in an Uxbridge industrial estate has certainly seen better days. We spend the next week building a wall and putting in a door (the wrong way around) so we can actually lock our new 360° photography studio that is going to change the world. We worked hard, and within a year there were nine people working for the company; but the books were deep in the red. We paid our employees on the last Friday of every month, and on one of those Fridays James walks in carrying a big box. At this point I've worked with him long enough to know that I should check our bank account – and sure enough, there's £10,000 less than there was the day before, and we're even further in the red on the day the staff need to be paid. "No problem," he says, patting the top of the box, "this is going to be the solution". I've heard this several times before, and I know that it means he's invested our salary money in expensive, non-essential equipment again. I knew it was time to leave.

I packed up my life in London and moved back to Norway, where I invested everything I owned in a carbon copy of the business James and I had been running in the UK. I convinced myself that, however much of a failure the first attempt had been, I was not a quitter and that I would never ever *ever* give up, because the only way to fail is to give up without learning from your mistakes and trying again. It also helped that I knew how to run a photography business at this point, so it seemed like the best chance to make a large amount of money in a short amount of time – and at that point in my life, making copious amounts of money was pretty much my only goal. I had a product that was unique and that my former customers in the UK had loved; I had a business model that was cheap to run and turned a good profit; and I had experience of running a company. What could possibly go wrong?

Well, on the business side of things, not a lot – my new business started to make a bit of money, and the clients were increasing as the months went on. But as the sole operator of the business, I was getting increasingly stressed out and working long hours just to get everything done on time. Sure, I was making money, but I had no time for anything but work, and the stress of employees, accounting, marketing, and wondering if I could pay our bills next month was making my life more and more difficult. I was in physical and emotional pain, and I started drinking too much – it started with a shot of Jack Daniels before bed, just to help me get to sleep; then moved up to two; and before I knew it I needed half a bottle just to calm me down enough to sleep through the night. On the inside those were dark and painful days – but on the surface, everything looked good, and if I could just keep going I'd come out on the other side with a profitable business and everything would be fine, right?

# Memento Mori

*ExCel Centre, London, October* 2010 – I'm in a conference hall in central London, attending an event with a name that suggests I have it all – the National Achievers Congress. That's what I am, an achiever – I own businesses, I make money, I attend conferences for people that want to become rich and wealthy like this one. That's what achievers do. But something's not quite right. I have a strange feeling in my chest, like someone's sitting on me and stopping me from breathing properly. It must just be some fresh air that I need, I've been inside this building all day, chatting to people, sending emails on my smartphone, I just need to relax a little bit, have a rest for a few minutes.

So I head outside and lie down on the grass next to the conference center for a little while. I try to zone out, concentrate on something else other than this weird feeling that won't go away. I try to focus on other things. I try to focus on nothing. I look at the sky. I look at the grass. Nothing works, all I can think about is this pain. I don't feel well at all, I should go home, take the rest of the day off, hopefully it'll pass over within a few hours and I can get back to work tomorrow. I crawl to my feet and shuffle off to the nearest tube station, feeling like crap.

I haven't timed this very well. It's rush hour, on the tube, in central London. Standing room only. Barely even room to turn around. And this numbness and dizziness, whatever it is, is getting worse. I look down, and my hands look really...strange. Pale, a sort of white color, tinged with blue. I look back up and everything spins a little – I won't be looking down again, I'm way too dizzy. My heart is pounding – I can't think straight enough to count right now, but it feels like two hundred beats a minute. That can't be right. That's not how hearts are supposed to work, even in a rush hour tube. Everything's still spinning, stay still, stay still – I start to wobble, and fall, and I grab the arm of the person next to me, and manage to plead, gasping for breath, "get me out of here".

God bless that man, because he took the time out of his own life to get me to a hospital, which was a very important place for me to go because I was having a major panic attack. As we sat in the ambulance on the way to Accident & Emergency, however, I thought it was even worse than that – I thought I was going to die. I rang my partner up, and with what I thought were my last breaths, I gave her instructions – the passwords to my various business email accounts, the details of who should be in charge of everything when I'm gone, who should inherit these various business systems that I'd built up over the years. I spent the rest of the day attached to various monitors while the doctors ensured I was fine, and I was put under strict orders to relax and not to do any work for the next few weeks.

Let's skip in time again, to the present day. I'm happy and healthy. In my best months, I make $20,000 from 20-40 hours of work on my three businesses, which I operate primarily through outsourcing and licensing to others. I have the free time to travel around the world, keep myself fit, and eat well. I split my time between London, Oslo, San Francisco, and Davao City in the Philippines. Most importantly, I'm completely changed from that stressed out, panicked man who lay on the grass outside a conference center in London a few short years ago. Importantly, I'm also changed from that bored man who sat alone in a beachside restaurant in Malibu.

What happened? At the time of my panic attack, I thought I was going to die. After that, as I recovered, I realized that I was right – I am going to die, one day, and there's no way to predict what day it will be. It could be tomorrow, it could be fifty years from now. In the moment when I thought it was all going to end I was left with a feeling that I had not completed my mission in life; and that if I lived, I would first figure out what my purpose was, and then I would commit to living it. I realized that time is the only commodity that we all start out with equal amounts of, and the only commodity that you can't get anymore of. You can't go to a shop and buy more time. So I knew at that point that I needed to ensure my life, my limited amount of time on this earth, wasn't wasted.

So I focused wholeheartedly on my businesses for a while, coming up with more and more ideas for making money. But it wasn't until Malibu that I realized I still hadn't got the balance right. I had been focused on money and business, and I suddenly knew that those were not my purpose in life – they were just mechanisms to provide the security needed to really follow my dreams and desires. My panic attack had given me the gift of time, by making me understand how little of it I had left, but I was still misusing that time to focus single-mindedly on work, rather than on the experiences and the people I loved. I had not been liberated from working – I had simply become more efficient at it.

I had thought that by focusing on business and money I was making myself free, but I didn't understand that freedom requires more balance than that. At that point I knew that if I was going to truly be free, if I was really going to be liberated from work, I needed to focus on ways to reduce the amount of time I spent maintaining my business, and to increase the amount of time I had to focus on what I should really be doing with my life. I knew then that freedom is not just going towards what you think will give you the most lavish lifestyle – freedom is doing and going towards what you love.

And that's what I want to talk to you about.

## Never Work Again

Welcome to a very different kind of business book. The title of this book is *Never Work Again*, and in many ways that's exactly what it's about – how you can run a business that ensures you don't end up feeling like I did on that tube train a few years ago. A business that makes you money without taking up every spare second of your time, every last morsel of your thought and energy, every last ounce of your soul. A business that gives you the time to work on your own passions in life, and doesn't feel like a chore every time you're required to give your attention to it. In short, a business that allows you to work less while earning more.

But, at the same time as providing practical guidance – taken from my own experience – on  setting up such a business, this book will also encourage you to explore some more philosophical questions. The kind of questions I think need to be addressed if you are going to live a life of freedom. In particular, what does freedom mean to you? People, and especially those opportunity-seeking entrepreneurs, often think about freedom purely in terms of money, and I'm going to be encouraging you to take a different approach from now on – to think about freedom in less material terms, to think about money as merely a necessary mechanism for allowing you to follow your true passions, and to define clearly what those passions are so that you can live out your purpose.

Ultimately, the aim of this book is to help you become a successful entrepreneur – to share in the benefits of the knowledge I've amassed over years of trial and error, and to avoid the pitfalls that I faced of working too hard and stressing too much. Having overcome those problems, I now have a passion for helping other people who might end up going the same way – budding entrepreneurs such as yourself – and that's what led me to writing this book.

The things I'm going to show you in this book are the things that you don't learn in school. School doesn't prepare you for the life of being an entrepreneur, it doesn't give you the skills and the mindset you need. School teaches you to be an employee, to follow orders, to work for someone else. Being an entrepreneur is the absolute opposite of this – you're in charge and you need to take advantage of the opportunities presented to you. Usually, this means a lot of trial and error – but if you're reading this book you'll be getting a headstart on everyone else because I'll be sharing what I already know about the process. I've already made the painful mistakes, so you don't have to.

## Who Is This Book For?

There are four levels of entrepreneurship, and if you're in any of the first three levels, this book can be a big help to you. On the first level we have 'wantrepreneurs' – these are the people that want to start their own business, but they haven't gotten around to it yet. I have two key pieces of advice for these people before we even begin – firstly, you need to decide if you really want to be an entrepreneur or whether you just *think* you want to be an entrepreneur. I got my first job at the age of 14, because the idea of making my own money was so appealing to me even then; and as I've described above, my boss in the brand consultancy could see I was clearly not meant to be an employee. Some people, however, while they fantasize about being a Richard Branson-style entrepreneur, are not really cut out for it – they might try it out, but they pretty quickly realize that they prefer the security and the routine of a regular job. That's fine, I'm not saying there's anything wrong with that – although it's not for me – but you need to give a bit of thought to whether you're really an entrepreneur at heart.

Maybe read some more of the book, and as I talk more about what entrepreneurship involves, you'll know whether it's for you.

The second piece of advice I want to give to wantrepreneurs right now is – just do it! The sooner you start, the sooner you'll begin learning about the ins and outs of running your own business, and the sooner you'll get to the point where you never need to work again. So read through the book, where you'll find a lot of ideas for potential business models and techniques that you can apply to cut down your working time, and then get going – by the time you reach the end of the book, you'll be ready for action.

The second level of entrepreneurship is what I call 'solopreneurs'. These people have already started their own business, but they're currently the only person working for it – they're basically self-employed. They tend to be taking on literally every role in a business, no matter how suited they are for it – marketing, networking, accounting, admin, and so on. The key for solopreneurs is delegating and outsourcing, letting other people take the strain for them, and becoming more efficient and more profitable in the process. This is what I call leveraging other people's time – it's what successful business owners do, and it's what I'm going to show you to do in order to reduce your own working time to a minimum. The second action a solopreneur needs to take to achieve their freedom is to start selling a product, instead of a service. That doesn't necessarily mean making a product from scratch or having to invent something new, but products are far easier to scale and sell than services.

On the third level we have operators. Operators own a bigger business than a solopreneur – they have employees and offices and are usually fairly well-established. But they have no free time whatsoever, because even though they have other people doing the little tasks for them, they always need to be around to make sure everything goes smoothly. If they take a week off, the business starts falling apart – and if the operator doesn't get back to work soon, the business will die. The big problem they have is a lack of automation and systems thinking – their business requires them to be around all the time in order to make sure things are working, and this means that they end up with a business that owns them, rather than the other way round. We'll be discussing a lot more about automation in chapter six.

My aim is to try and get all of you – whichever of those three levels you're on – to the fourth level, which is being a business owner. What's the difference between being a business operator and a business owner? An operator needs to be constantly involved in order to make sure things are, well, operating. A business owner owns a system, but he doesn't operate it on a daily basis – he has other people to do that, and he knows that his business system is set up in a way that will allow it to carry on even if he is not around. He makes himself an inessential part of the system, while still owning it and therefore making the most profit out of it – and in doing so, he gives himself a huge amount of free time in comparison to the other three levels. That's what I do – I own businesses, they don't own me. I work around twenty hours a month – that's roughly one hour of work a day – and I sometimes make as much as $20,000 a month. And that's because I *own* a system that doesn't need me to be present to *operate* it. And if I can do it, you can do it.

# The Four Levels Of Entrepreneurs

What kind of entrepreneur are you?

### Level One - Wantrepreneur

Always got lots of ideas, but never takes action. Never gets anything off the ground, but that's ok because they have a new and better idea lined up. We are all entrepreneurs at heart, but school teaches us not to be. This is where most people end their entrepreneurial thoughts.

### Level Two - Solopreneur

Invests in their education, registers a business and starts taking some form of action, but they don't get any sales and get talked out of their business by their friends and family. They own a JOB and do everything. Doctors, dentists and lawyers are mostly placed in this category.

### Level Three - Operator

Has an idea, goes and gets educated, invests in himself and starts generating money. Sales and business are going well, but suddenly you realize that you are stuck in your business and the business owns you not the other way around.

### Level Four - Owner

Highest level of entrepreneurship and this is where you need to be if you want freedom from your business. You are allowed to focus on the parts of your business that you love and the freedom that comes with this kind of lifestyle.

*Source: The Four Levels of Entrepreneurs (Bakke, 2013)*
www.**youwillneverworkagain**.com

More generally, this book is aimed at anyone who is interested in business but also interested in living a good life, a life of freedom, a life where you have both the time and money to follow your heart and live your purpose.

That's the meaning of *Never Work Again* – not to achieve a life of vegging out in front of the television or working on your tan on a yacht in the Mediterranean (not that there's anything wrong with that, *per se*), but to create massive value in the world by finding your quest and living out its purpose, and to follow your passions, interests, and desires.

## The Layout of This Book

This book is split roughly into four parts. In the first part we explore what freedom really means, and the idea of living your life in freedom rather than being a slave to your business. Using examples from literature, religion, psychology, and my own life, we'll discuss the fact that death is inevitable, and why realizing and understanding that fact should spur you to make changes in your life (I know, exactly what you expected from a business book, right?). We'll look at the social programming that conditions us all from birth to be greedy, lazy, and constantly chasing after money – you might think chasing after money is the sign of a good businessman, but I'll explain that this is not always true, and that true success follows very different principles. Most importantly, though, this first section will look at the idea that everyone has a "true path" in life which needs to be followed – a set of passions or desires, often obscured by social programming, which for entrepreneurs is usually related to greed, sloth, and pride. We'll look at some ways in which you can start to identify that true path, giving you the first step on the way to freedom and happiness in business. This first part of the book is ideal for anyone who feels trapped by their life or their business, and wants to consider some of the big issues that lie behind that unhappiness and some of the ways of alleviating it. Why am I starting the book with this philosophical inquiry? Because I think it's important that we start at our end point – if you want to achieve freedom, you need to understand what freedom is before you set off towards it, rather than spending thousands of hours pursuing something you don't really understand. As Stephen Covey said in *The Seven Habits of Highly Effective People*, you need to "start with the end in mind". These two chapter also act as motivation, to get you into the right mindset to succeed.

The second part of the book is aimed at people who are just starting out in entrepreneurship – you're full of ideas, energy, and enthusiasm, but you don't have a concrete, functioning business yet. This section provides a number of no money down, outsourceable blueprints for some of the business models that I have found to be most successful in my own life – business models that, once they are set up and refined to ensure they are running well, will allow you to take the free time you need to explore your true path and your deeper desires without constantly being bogged down by must-do "work stuff". These models allow you to outsource and automate much of the time-consuming or boring labor, allowing you to retain your sanity and free time, and to focus on high-level thinking, income generating activities, and building relationships with friends, family and business contacts.

The third part of the book is aimed at entrepreneurs who already have their business set up, but who feel trapped by it. We'll explore some of the ways in which you can refine your business systems, primarily through two techniques – automation and outsourcing. Automation is the creation of a system that runs like clockwork, even – and this is very important – when you remove yourself from it. Having a business system that requires you to constantly be present to ensure it doesn't fall apart is enslavement; owning a business system that continues to operate while you're doing other things is your duty as an entrepreneur – because it ensures that the value you're creating in the world lives on after you're gone.

The other major technique we'll discuss is outsourcing – hiring people from countries other than your own to work in your business. I'll explain the advantages of outsourcing, the particular jobs that can be outsourced, and provide you with examples of the specific details of organizing an outsourced business. Outsourcing has often received bad press in recent years, with various large corporations being accused of exploiting workers in developing countries. That's not the kind of outsourcing we're talking about in this book though – while one of the great advantages of outsourcing is that you'll be paying your employees less than if you hired in the US or western Europe, you must always treat others as you'd want to be treated yourself, and pay a fair and equitable wage. If done right, with humanity and genuine care for your employees, outsourcing can be a vital way of transferring value – in terms of money, security, and long-term knowledge and skills – to countries that need it more than our own. I'm going to suggest outsourcing much of your work to the Philippines, where you'll find that your employees are friendlier, more polite, more punctual, and more appreciative of the work than many of those in the western world.

The final part of the book acts as a conclusion, drawing together everything we have discussed in the other three parts, and discussing how the lessons learned in this book can be applied in your own life and can help you in your quest for freedom and your efforts to walk along and stay on your own true path.

## How to Use This Book

There are a number of different ways in which you can use this book. Some people will choose to simply read it right the way through, from beginning to end, and that's fine – if you're relatively new to being an entrepreneur, I'd even say that it's the ideal way to do it, and you'll hopefully pick up some of the philosophies, techniques, and ideas and use them in your business. Others who are more experienced or who already know that they have an interest in a particular topic or technique might want to be more selective with how they read the book, focusing on the chapters on automation and outsourcing, or on finding your own true path, for example.

Throughout the book there are a number of exercises designed to make you experience and understand some of the things we're talking about – these are, of course, optional, but I know from my own experiences that learning by doing is the best way to really understand something new, so I would encourage you to at least give them a go – they could be just the thing you need to find your true path.

Some of you will be reading this book as part of one of my online or offline training courses (and for more information about those, check out the back of the book), and we'll be working through these exercises during those courses – but feel free to take the time to familiarize yourself with them beforehand if you'd like. I want to emphasize how important it is to actually take action in order to learn. According to the 'learning cone' developed by Edgar Dale, we only remember about 10% of what we read. Bearing in mind that statistically only 3% of the people reading this book will take any action, the chances for success just through reading are very slim. On the other hand, we remember 90% of what we do – things that we take action on, rather than just reading about. It's only through doing the exercises and taking the actions that true learning comes and you will grow to your potential.

# Cone of Learning

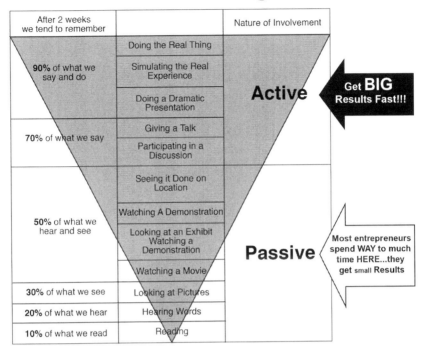

*Source: Cone of Learning adapted from (Dale, 1969)*

With all of that said, it's time to get started on finding your path, freeing your life, and never working again.

# CHAPTER 2

# Freedom or Death

*"The fear of death follows from the fear of life. A man who lives fully is prepared to die at any time."*

~Mark Twain

## Ancient Wisdom

In Nepal, in the 6th century BCE, there was a prince who lived a very sheltered life. His father made sure he lived in luxury, with everything he could ever want, and he never experienced or even heard about things like sickness, old age, death, or suffering. The prince, however, became curious about the world outside his royal compound, and one day disguised himself and went on a journey into the city, to see how the people he was born to rule lived their lives. He saw, at the side of the road, an old man hobbling forward slowly on a pair of decaying wooden crutches, stopping every few feet to let out a bone-shaking cough. He saw a beggar sitting next to the gutter, his skin covered in sores. And, he saw, at the edge of a field, a corpse – a man, dead, with no family to bury him, left on a grass verge and forgotten. Suddenly, all those things – old age, disease, death – became very real to him, he understood that they happen to all people and they would happen to him as well, and in that same instant he knew what he must do with the rest of his life.

That prince was Siddhartha Gautama, or as we more commonly know him, the Buddha, and he was not the only person to have this realization of the inevitability of death, disease, and suffering. It's a common theme in art and literature. Hubert Selby, Jr., the author of books including *Last Exit to Brooklyn* and *Requiem for a Dream*, once explained in an interview why he began to write. He had been very sickly and ill for much of his life up to that point, and said that he was sitting in his living room one day when a sudden realization hit him - "I knew that someday I was going to die. And I knew that before I died, two things would happen to me. Number one, I would regret my entire life, and number two, I would want to live my life over again". Luckily for him, he realized this while he still had time, and he went on to become one of the most infamous writers of fiction in the second half of the twentieth century.

The title character in Leo Tolstoy's short novel *The Death of Ivan Ilyich* was not so lucky. While hanging up the curtains in his fancy new house, Ivan Ilyich Golovin injures his side and, despite his previous good health, finds himself deteriorating until the doctors finally tell him that he is dying. He faces death in a terrified manner, screaming and screaming, pitying himself; until, one hour before the end, his moment of clarity comes, and he sees that he has spent his life living for himself and not for others – he realizes, so to speak, that he's been living in a mindset of 'me thinking', when he should have been doing 'we thinking'. There is some hope left for Ivan Ilyich though – having finally faced the inevitability of death, and having understood how he should have lived his life, he appears to die. As he closes his eyes, he hears someone around the bed say "he's gone", and with his final breath he whispers to himself, "death has gone".

We're conditioned to think about death as a bad thing. Something mysterious, dark, terrifying. Something we need to avoid or to put off for as long as possible. We buy all sorts of medicines and other treatments to try and hold off the inevitable – we buy tons of cosmetics and anti-aging creams to try and avoid even looking like we're getting older and closer to death. But ultimately, to paraphrase the old saying, the only thing more inevitable than taxes is death. But while we still might be unhappy about the fact that we're going to die, the understanding of that fact can be the spur to great actions – to improving our own lives and the lives of others around us, or finding our true path in life, like I did on the tube in London. It inspired me to create a 'bucket list' – a list of over a thousand things that I want to do before I die (I regularly add updates on my progress to my Youtube channel at https://www.youtube.com/erlendbakkeTV, and I explain more about making your own bucket list at www.youwillnever workagain.com/bonus). At the very least, understanding the reality of death can inspire us to live each day to the fullest and not waste a single minute.

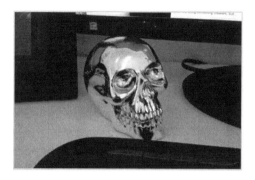

It's for that reason that I keep a skull on my desk at all time – a *memento mori*, or a reminder of mortality. I don't walk around actively reminiscing with my skull, like Shakespeare's Hamlet did, but its constant presence reminds me of my own near-death experience, and helps me stay focused on the way I want to live, rather than wasting time or procrastinating. Making things visible leads to action, and the constant visibility of death right in front of me is a key part of making sure I live the way I want to live and take the actions I want to take. It reminds me to ensure that I am continually growing as a person – as Lou Holz said, "In this world, you're either growing or you're dying".

So congratulations – you're going to die one day, and you have absolutely no way of knowing which day it will be. Maybe you'll get hit by a bus tomorrow. Maybe you'll live to be over a hundred years old. The point is that you will die, and realizing this – not just understanding it intellectually, but really, deep down, *knowing it* – should be the thing that encourages you to evaluate your life, the direction it's going in, and the things you want from it.

# Exercise: *The Funeral Exercise*
*(By Jakob Løvstad,* http://www.insightconsulting.no/en/*)*

*I learned this powerful exercise on clarity when attending Jakob Løvstad's six-month coaching course, Coach Craft. I strongly recommend this course to all leaders, entrepreneurs and people in general because if you think about it, we are always coaching each other anyway, so why not be great at it?*

*We never know when our final day will come - when I had my panic attack on the tube in London, I thought that was it, I was done for, and it happened so suddenly that I was not prepared. So this exercise will help you live life at a level that is worthy of you, and stay on that track until the fateful day comes.*

*You can either do this exercise with other people or alone. I strongly recommend gathering 2-4 friends and have them sit in front of you for the duration of 'your funeral'. This makes it a much more immersive experience and much more real. When I did the exercise at Coach Craft I thought to myself "I've got this, this'll be easy", but I ended up crying because my life purpose and quest became so much clearer to me. For such a long time I had read every book and gone to every course to find answers, but until I did this exercise my mission was foggy and unclear. One of the outcomes of the exercise for me is this very book, and my mission and duty to help liberate entrepreneurs like yourself through the course Work Less, Earn More.*

*Now to the exercise:*

1) *Find a piece of paper and a pen.*

2) *Draw two lines down the middle of the paper so it´s divided in 3 parts. Write 'Family', 'Friends', and 'Colleagues' above the different columns.*

3) *Find a quiet space, and put your timer on 10-15 minutes. Think of people in these three categories and write down what you think they would say about you if you were dead. Listen to your heart and try not to think so much, but write down what first comes into your head.*

4) *Once you have spent 10-15 minutes writing down the speeches, give them to your family, friends and colleagues to read aloud. Each person should stand up and give the speech in front of everybody else.*

5) *Listen to what you feel when doing this exercise and try to be as truthful as possible.*

---

**Check out the online video version of this exercise at**
http://youwillneverworkagain.com/exercises/

---

## Money – The Root of All Happiness?

This probably seems like a very odd way of opening a book about business. You're not reading this book to hear about death. You're reading a book called *Never Work Again* because you want to make more money while doing the least amount of work possible. You want the shortcut tips to living the rest of your life on a Caribbean island, being served vibrantly-colored cocktails by girls in grass skirts, while your business magically sends a non-stop supply of money to your bank account because you read a few hundred pages of a book and put a few simple suggestions into practice.

Sorry. Tony Robbins has said that success is 80% psychology and 20% strategy, and this is the psychology part. One of the 'seven habits of highly effective people' is to start with the end in mind, and that's also what we're doing here. Because your end goal, even if it's just to make a huge amount of money, is essentially psychological – you want to be happy.

We are conditioned to believe that money and material possessions are the root of our happiness. Owning more stuff and having more money will make us more happy and let us feel more free. After all, people with more money than us can do whatever they want, right? Isn't that what freedom is? And there's always stories in the newspapers of self-made millionaires who designed a new iPhone app or discovered the killer product that everyone wants and who never need to work again – those people must have the most freedom of all, just a little bit of luck and a smattering of work at the beginning, and now they have cars, houses, permanent vacations on that grass-skirted paradise island. Luxury. If only we had the same amount of money.

In actual fact, things aren't quite as simple as that. If money and material goods were the key to happiness, we'd never see either of those two famous archetypes, the 'poverty stricken family who can barely afford two sticks to rub together but they're happy because they have each other', and the 'stressed out businessman who drives a Porsche and has a nice apartment but is still having a panic attack on the tube'. You might remember that last one from the previous chapter. Having money didn't seem to help me much back then.

Let's have a look at a very famous diagram – Abraham Maslow's hierarchy of needs (which I also discuss in a free YouTube tutorial at www.youwillneverworkagain.com/bonus). You've almost certainly seen this before, but I'll quickly talk you through it. Maslow argues that there are five levels of human needs, represented by a pyramid structure. At the bottom of the pyramid are the needs which are seen as more 'basic', but which must be fulfilled first before we move up the pyramid. This includes air, food, water, sex, and sleep – if we haven't got enough of these needs, we'll go looking for them before we worry about anything else. The second level is safety and security; the third is love and belonging; the fourth is self-esteem, confidence, and the respect of others; and the very top level is what Maslow called self-actualization – that is, the realization of our full potential through creativity, problem solving, and understanding.

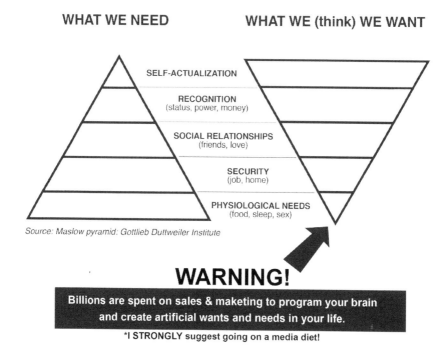

**WHAT WE NEED**          **WHAT WE (think) WE WANT**

SELF-ACTUALIZATION

RECOGNITION
(status, power, money)

SOCIAL RELATIONSHIPS
(friends, love)

SECURITY
(job, home)

PHYSIOLOGICAL NEEDS
(food, sleep, sex)

Source: Maslow pyramid: Gottlieb Duttweiler Institute

**WARNING!**

Billions are spent on sales & maketing to program your brain
and create artificial wants and needs in your life.

*I STRONGLY suggest going on a media diet!

How does this relate to our desires for money and material wealth? We tend to think that wealth will make us happier because we need it to progress up the pyramid. Obviously, we need money to get food and shelter, fulfilling the first level. We use our money to go to level two and build safety and security for ourselves, buying a house rather than renting it, for example, ensuring that we won't end up living on the streets, back on the first level of the pyramid in the future. We have a house and some money, so we can afford to look after our loved ones, level three. And then, when we have enough money to be sure about the bottom three levels, we can start to really concentrate on level four – we can socialize in expensive bars with our colleagues, drive cars that we think will get us the respect and envy of other people, display our achievements in life through our conspicuous consumption. The fifth level? Well, we tend not to think about that one too much, it's a bit more complex. If we do consider it, we tend to take Maslow's description of level five – "what a man can be, he must be" – and twist it to assume that 'what a man can be' is defined in terms of 'what a man can earn and what a man can have', with our pride in our own possessions, titles, family name, golf clubs, and the like leading the way.

There are two obvious problems to this approach to the hierarchy of needs which focuses primarily on the fourth level. The first is that most of us are not actually very good at the first three levels. We don't get enough sleep because we're working twelve hour days trying to become richer and richer. We eat crappy food because we don't have the time or energy to prepare anything better, or even to educate ourselves about what might be better. We have families who love us, but we barely see them because of our pursuit of money – which, of course, we're only doing because we're thinking of them and their security, honest. Most of us have bad sex because our bodies are at breaking point and we don't have the time to form emotional connections with our partner. And we don't even feel security or safety with our money because we're always competing and comparing ourselves against others, or afraid that people are going to steal from us. We work to get all that money, and then we're paranoid about keeping it – it would almost be better just to not bother.

The second problem in our understanding of our needs is our attitude to the upper levels of the hierarchy. We think self-esteem comes from impressing other people with the things we own; and we think self-actualization means social climbing and consumption. Instead of defining who we are and what our potential is – the real meaning of self-actualization – we reduce ourselves to the things we own and we consider ourselves to be the sum of our material wealth. And this mindset makes us susceptible to the billions of dollars spent every year on advertising and media to create artificial needs – things that we think we need in order to progress up the pyramid, but which are really just distracting us from true self-actualization.

This is all a little abstract, so let me tell you a couple of stories to illustrate my point.

A few years ago I bought a Porsche. I'd always wanted a Porsche, it had been my goal for a long time, and I thought that once I had it, I'd be really happy – goal achieved. People would have more respect for me, I'd have more confidence, everyone would know that I had become 'what a man can be'. Because I owned a Porsche, and some companies, and all those other status symbols. Of course, that was a ridiculous assumption to make, and I realized that very quickly. I picked the car up from the airport and drove it downtown – this was around the time that the global financial crisis was heating up, and there was a demonstration in the city center. I happened to drive straight past the place where the protesters were gathered, still glowing with pride at my new purchase, still feeling like I was bound to get respect from everyone I met. And of course that was not the case – instead, I just got a whole load of middle fingers and a lot of abusive words.

Some people will say I should just have ignored it, that the protesters were just jealous of my success, but I think of it a different way. I realized that I was doing things because of the impact I thought it would have on other people – which is a ridiculous and insane habit, because you can't control what other people will think or say about you. Some people are always going to find a reason to hate you – sometimes they might have a point, sometimes they might not, but it's always going to happen. Think of it as the 'rule of three' for social interactions – one third of all the people who meet you will like you, one third will dislike you, and one third will be completely indifferent, and there's nothing you can do to significantly shift those numbers. So I understood that rather than doing things to impress other people, I needed to do them for myself. Owning a Porsche was nice, but I wasn't really a lot happier – the rest of my life was still just as much of a mess as it was before.

## My Millionaire Friend

A friend of mine lives out a similar experience. He's always been rich, he was fortunate enough to be the son of wealthy parents, and he inherited $20 million at the age of 18, an incredible sum of money. After I moved back to Oslo to start again from scratch, more ambitious and money hungry than ever, we went sailing – of course, he owns his own yacht – and I thought about all the advantages he seemed to have, all the stuff he owned, the life he was lucky enough to live. I mentioned this to him, how great his life seemed to be and how I wished I could afford my own yacht, and he turned to me and all he said was "your things own you". He's sold the boat since then, and moved into a fairly humble flat in Oslo. He tells me he's much happier this way, and I believe him. I've come to realize, through my own experience and seeing the experiences of others, that my self-worth and my net-worth are not the same thing.

Other, similar stories are easy to find, of people who, on the surface, appear to have it all – money, fame, possessions – but in private remain cripplingly unhappy and have a constant feeling of being unfulfilled. If you're reading this book, you might not be at that level of wealth yet, but you may be experiencing similar kinds of feelings. You own a business, but you feel trapped by it. You make some money, but you always feel under pressure to make more. As Tony Robbins says, "success without fulfillment is the ultimate failure". The 'more' mindset isn't freedom, it's captivity, because there is always somebody with a bigger boat or private jet than you.

## The Psychology of Things

> *"Those who control and use their own minds escape my web."*
>
> ~Napoleon Hill,
> *Outwitting the Devil: The Secret to Freedom and Success*

The constant desire for 'things', for material goods and money, is a symptom of the amount of focus we put on that rather shallow part of us that we might call the intellect, the mind, or the ego. Our intellect is great for solving problems, inventing things, and finding ingenious new ways of creating profit, but it isn't so great at determining what will make us happy. Instead, the mind determines that something is missing from our lives, that something is making us unhappy, and calculates that the best way to make us happy again is through buying and owning things. To our logical minds, this is the most efficient way of solving the problem – it's pretty easy to make a little money (or get some on credit) and spend it on some consumer item that we like the look of, and we do indeed get a little, short-term boost of dopamine, a chemical that makes us feel happy, when we buy things. It's almost the same reaction as our brain has on cocaine – probably why bankers are so in love with both of these things...

Ultimately though, conspicuous consumption and displays of wealth are just failed attempts by our ego to protect us from our vulnerabilities and the judgments of others. The ego – the little voice inside our heads, if you will – is supposed to protect our sense of self, to help us feel confident, to make sure we feel safe. But it's a strange and complicated phenomenon, and often ends up hurting us even when it's trying to help – in a modern world that's so based around consumption, our egos become convinced that the path to happiness and safety is to join in with that consumption, and so our egos end up judging us just as much as other people do, telling us to constantly buy more stuff and make more money. The ego thinks it's doing this for our own good, to win us the respect of other people and to make us into 'what a man can be' (which, you'll recall, tends be judged by 'what a man can own' in our society). Our mind doesn't realize that it's actually hurting us and making us even more unhappy.

"Jake: *You see, I find that everyone has a number and it's usually an exact number. So what's yours?*

Bretton James: *More.*"

~**Wall Street:** Money Never Sleeps (2010)

The psychological theories of the French philosopher Jacques Lacan can be an interesting way of thinking about why consumerism doesn't make us happy. Lacan argues that because our entire lives are mediated through thought and language, we cannot directly perceive *la réelle*, 'the real'. At the same time, we have an understanding, buried deep within ourselves, that there is something more 'real' beyond our current lives, but we don't know how to access it. This leaves us with a sense of emptiness and desire – but we don't really know or understand what it is we desire, because we don't really know or understand 'the real'. Instead, we displace our desire onto other things – particularly sex, money, and possessions. We think that getting these things will make us happy, but when we do get them we vaguely realize that they were, in fact, not the things we were looking for. But we still don't understand what we were really looking for, so we continue with the illusion that it must be money – we just don't have enough money yet to be happy! We just need to get some more, then we'll be there! And so the cycle continues, and we continue to be unhappy.

# *Exercise:* The Three Most Important Questions

*(By Vishen Lakhiani (http://www.mindvalley.com/goal-setting-redefined)*

*I strongly recommend downloading Mindvalley's* Omvana *app (http://www.omvana.com/) and listening to this meditation daily. You might be telling yourself "I don't have time for that". I used to never have time for little things like this either, but the secret to success is actually practicing these little habits that will counteract your programming every single day. What is more important than living the life that you want and should be living? Ask yourself, how can I do this 15 minute meditation daily? Can I listen to it on the bus? Replace another habit with it? 'How can I?' is the right question to ask yourself daily.*

> *"In the end, people either have excuses or experiences; reasons or results; buts or brilliance. They either have what they wanted or they have a detailed list of all the rational reasons why not."*
>
> ~Anonymous

*Chapter 3 talks more about how to train your brain through meditation practices such as; mindfulness, guided meditation, Reiki, Aikido, Qi Gong, and Tai Chi. I practice one or more of these every single day, and I decide what to practice based on how I feel rather than having a set system written in stone, because different days need slightly different rituals. Don't worry about this so much at this point, but I strongly encourage you to do the exercise below from Mindvalley before you continue.*

*"Over the years I've come to stop believing in goal setting. Why? Because goal setting, or at least the way most of us are trained to do it, actually gets us to be obsessed about the how of attaining our goals, rather than the passion, the vision, and the beauty of the goal itself. In short, we get obsessed with the 'means', rather than the 'end'. And this is why so many of us wake up at the age of 40 one day, dreading going to work because we were forced to pick a career before we could legally buy a beer.*

*In this exercise, we are going to change the way you think about goal setting. We are going to present to you the 3 most important questions to ask yourself. If everyone asked themselves these questions at the age of 18, the world would be a much happier place. But no matter how old you are, it's not too late. This exercise will change the way you plan your life and see your goals. It'll change the way you see your career, mission, and life purpose unfolding. The intro to the exercise takes no more than 5 minutes, and the exercise itself takes 7 minutes. This could be one of the most important 12 minutes of your life."*

*See more at:* http://www.mindvalley.com/goal-setting-redefined

---

**Take a look at my explanation of this exercise at**
http://youwillneverworkagain.com/exercises/

---

To actually become happy, you need to surrender your ego. This is difficult, because most of us don't even realize that we have an ego until we get broken down to the level where we need to go within and start to think about it, and consider why we make the decisions we make, and whether they are making us happy or unhappy. At that time it often becomes clear that, indeed, we do have an ego, and the ego is making a lot of our decisions for us without us necessarily thinking things through in their totality.

And this leads us back to death. Steve Jobs, in his 2005 commencement address at Stanford University, said that 'everything falls away in the face of death', leaving only the truly important things behind it. Pride, greed, lust and – most importantly – the ego disappear, and you are left with an understanding of what you love. Of course, the ideal situation is to achieve this before the point at which we are facing death, so we can live out our purpose doing what we love – so now is the ideal time to start looking. In the same speech, Jobs also said "I was lucky — I found what I loved to do early in life...you've got to find what you love...if you haven't found it yet, keep looking" – good advice indeed. Similarly, Lacan said that we cannot access or understand 'the real', the great totality of life, and he may be right – but we can access the totality of ourselves, and understand not just 'what a man can be', but what *we* can be, what our true and complete self involves, rather than simply following the demands of our conditioning and ego. In doing this, we can start to have a new relationship with money, time, and the people around us.

"The Ego Trap

1. *Having high self-esteem has a few modest benefits, but it can produce problems and is mostly irrelevant for success.*

2. *The pursuit of self-esteem through a focus on greatness makes us emotionally vulnerable to life's disappointments and can even lower our chances of success.*

3. *Compassion, along with a less self-centered perspective, can motivate us to achieve while helping us weather bad news, learn from our mistakes and fortify our friendships."*

~Jennifer Crocker, Professor, Ohio State University

## Clarity and Balance

Now, let me clear about something here. I'm an entrepreneur. I make money from running businesses. Despite what you might think from the previous few pages, I am NOT trying to tell you that you shouldn't make money, or even that you shouldn't want to make money. What I am trying to do is to encourage a recalibration of our relationship with money. For too many businessmen and entrepreneurs, money is an obsession. It's the only goal they have, the only way they think their lives can be measured and accounted for. I'm trying to explain to you that while money is important, it isn't the only thing that's important.

As we've seen above, it's the brain, the intellectual mind, the ego – whatever you want to call it – that leads us to fixate on money. Freedom is not going to come just by focusing on that part of ourselves. Instead, we need to be able to focus on listening to our heart and our instinctual desires as well – our gut feeling, if you will, for what is right, what is wrong, and what will make us happy. This means taking the time to sit down, relax, and explore what it is that we really want from life – it can't just be money, money is just pieces of paper in your wallet, or ones and zeros on a computer screen. Money is the thing that allows us to follow our heart, to focus on our true passions – the thing that allows us to feel secure and safe in our lives so that we no longer have to focus on basic survival – but money isn't valuable in itself. It's only valuable when we use it to get the things and the experiences we really want, so rather than chasing endless amounts of money, you should think about what your 'freedom number' is – the amount of money that you need to live life the way you want. This will be enough to cover your fixed costs, like rent, insurance, mobile phone contracts; and also your variable costs, like going out, taking lessons in new skills you want to learn, traveling and having new experiences, and so on. On top of that, you should always be aiming to have an extra 10% on top of what you need to invest in a passive income stream like an index fund. So your number needs to be able to cover the lifestyle you want to lead – if you make more than that without sacrificing yourself, that's great! But if you reach the right number to live the lifestyle you want, and find that the only way to make more is to sacrifice that lifestyle, then you should think carefully about whether you want to do that – after all, your money is only really useful as a key to opening up the life you want.

What is your true desire? Siddhartha Gautama realized his true desire, his calling in life, was to eliminate suffering from his own life, and to teach others to do the same. Your true calling doesn't need to be quite so high-minded though. Hubert Selby, Jr. had his moment of revelation in his living room, and dedicated himself to writing. You may find, when you look within yourself, that you want to do the same. You may find that you want to spend more time with your family and friends. You may want to travel the world, work out more often, buy a Harley Davidson and spend your time in the garage tinkering with it. The options are endless.

And all of them require at least some money. But, and here is the important thing, they *are not money*. By following your passion in this manner, you are allowing your intellectual side and your instinctual, emotional side to work together – start by following your heart and allowing it to guide you in finding the things you want to do, then use your mind to monetize the process and make money from doing what you love. The end result is that you're bringing in money, while following your passion. The mind is now working to achieve the goals that the heart has set; rather than the usual situation, where the heart is subdued in favor of the mind, and we end up chasing after more and more for its own sake.

Instead of chasing after money simply for the sake of having more, ask yourself 'what's my number?'. There's a scene in the movie Wall Street 2 in which a character is asked 'what's your number', and simply replies, with a smirk, 'more'. That's the kind of thinking a lot of entrepreneurs have, but I'm going to encourage you to be a bit more specific – ask yourself 'what is the least amount of money I need to live the life that I want to lead?'. We do things backwards in the West at the moment – we seem to have decided that we should make the money first, then design the ideal lifestyle afterwards. It's time to flip that around – work out how you want to live your life first, then work out how much money it's going to take, then only work the number of hours you need to reach that number. For example, I've decided that $20,000 a month is the right number for me – that's all I need to live the lifestyle I want while also saving something for my later years. I can often make that money by working 20-40 hours a month. If I doubled my work hours I could probably make $40,000 faster, but why would I? My businesses are compounding based on their systems and habits so I will naturally make $40,000 a month soon enough, but I'm in no rush to make more just for the sake of it. I'd be giving up my free time, the time that I use to actually live the lifestyle I want, in exchange for money that I don't need (not to mention that once your company is successful, success tends to compound and your profits will likely grow without needing to increase your workload). That's the kind of mindset I want you to start thinking with because you will start focusing less on money and more on the game of business and the beauty of seeing how a business can work without you.

The key word is *balance*. We've spent most of this chapter focusing on the problem of being too fixated on money, on the ego, on the intellect, because that's a much more common problem in contemporary society. And that fixation has left us with an unbalanced society – we've neglected social programs, community spirit, and the environment in favor of a single-minded focus on money. But equally, it's possible to go to far the other way – while I think the Buddha was an extraordinary man, I think it would be going too far to suggest that everyone throw away all of their possessions and wander into the woods to start leading an ascetic lifestyle. Too much focus on the heart can lead to a detachment from the world, and even a feeling of apathy, and that's not something I want to encourage either. Luckily, that problem is much less common in our society. What we do need, however, is to swing the scales a little bit more towards a focus on the heart rather than the brain, to emotions rather than ego, to our true desires rather than our marketing-induced wants – to create a sense of balance between our businesses and our lives. Traditionally we are taught to make decisions based on our thinking, rather than our feeling. What I'm suggesting here is that we change the hierarchy from the mind being the boss and the heart the slave. Instead listen to your heart first, making it the boss, and execute with the brain, making it your slave. That is the surest way to start living the life you truly desire.

## Brain/Heart Hierarchy

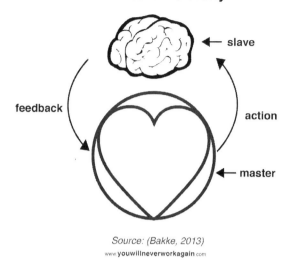

*Source: (Bakke, 2013)*
www.youwillneverworkagain.com

Let me give you a concrete example of what I mean by balance, and how it applies to what I'm going to talk about in the rest of the book. I have a friend who is a lawyer. He earns roughly as much as I do, but when I ring him up to see if he wants to go for a drink or go windsurfing or take a trip somewhere for the weekend, he always has to tell me 'sorry Erlend, I'm working'. I work twenty hours a month – he works three times that *every week*. Two things are clear here. The first is that although we make the same amount of money in total, I make a much better hourly rate, or as Tim Ferris would put it, I have a better 'relative income' – if I'm working twenty hours a month and making $20,000, that's $1,000 an hour; he makes the same, but with as many as 240 hours a month, which is only $83 an hour. Still a decent wage, but I know which hourly rate I prefer – and it's my aim to set you in the direction of making that kind of hourly rate in the rest of this book. And this leads on to the second thing – I clearly have a better work-life balance. My schedule of 'things I have to do to make money' is light, and I have the spare time to take up opportunities as they come, and to follow my heart and my passions.

An interesting side effect of starting to listen to your heart is that you not only start to see your own life differently – your whole view of the world starts to change as well. With less focus on the wants of the ego, we start to think less in terms of 'me me me', and more in terms of 'we' and 'us', about the ways in which various problems in our lives or our societies can be altered, about the ways in which you can give value back to the world. This is what I call an 'entrepreneur mindset'.

> *"My income is in direct proportion to my ability to add massive and measurable levels of value to other human beings."*
>
> ~Mark Anastasi

This might surprise some people, as we tend to assume that entrepreneurs are hard-nosed businessmen who are only after money and who would throw their own grandmother under a speeding train if it would help them succeed. But that's a bit unfair. In reality, true entrepreneurs are people who identify problems and solve them. We might not think of Mark Zuckerberg as a particularly altruistic individual, but he spotted a problem – the difficulty of keeping connected with the many people you meet on a college campus, and the difficulties of organizing and publicizing events – and he came up with a system to make it easier. The same goes for most other inventors and entrepreneurs throughout history – da Vinci, Edison, Jobs – all of them were looking for solutions to problems. True entrepreneurs don't just think about themselves, they think about what is most useful and valuable to society, because they know that creating things of value is the best way to receive value in return – it's simple business sense, much more so than the 'greed is good' individualism that is often promoted as the way to succeed and live a fulfilled life. The value that entrepreneurs create can continue even when they're gone – if they build their ideas into an automated system like the ones I'm going to talk about later, the value they create continues to exist even if something happens to them. The way to think about whether you're in the right place is to ask yourself what would happen to your business if you lost both of your arms tomorrow – does the value you've created in the world continue to exist and grow? Or is the business essentially over? While it sounds strange, to truly create value in the world, you need to make yourself dispensable in your business.

Ultimately, the aim of the rest of this book is to show you how to be an entrepreneur who values freedom, and who puts emphasis on the 'we' rather than just the 'me'. To show you how to run a business that you enjoy being a part of and which allows you to have the spare time to develop your intellectual, emotional, spiritual and physical interests. And to give you an idea of how to find the clarity you need to follow your own true path in life.

Nobody ever lay on their death bed and wished they had made an extra dollar. Remember that when you're prioritizing things – making money is good, but living life is better. As a final example of this, Mike Michalowicz, author of *The Toilet Paper Entrepreneur*, has said that the final words of Sam Walton, the founder of Walmart and one of the world's richest men, were simply: "I blew it". As he lay dying, surrounded by the family he never had the time to truly enjoy, one of the richest, most successful men in the world knew that he'd done things wrong.

## So What is Freedom?

I've spent a lot of this chapter discussing what freedom isn't. Now let's end by briefly discussing what freedom *is*. The problem is that, in many ways, it's difficult to come up with a single definition of freedom. As I'll discuss in the next chapter, the exact details of what freedom means can and should differ from person to person. However, there are a few things I can say.

There are five kinds of freedom, and they form a hierarchy a little like Maslow's pyramid. There is political freedom, the freedom that underlies all of our actions – the freedom to write whatever we want, say whatever we want, and believe whatever we want. There is social freedom, the freedom to live our daily lives and have relationships with whoever we choose, without being abused or harassed. There is financial freedom, the idea of which I've already discussed quite a lot in this chapter.

And then there are the two most advanced forms of freedom. Freedom of the mind is the freedom to give up the ego and its fear, its controlling manner, and its insecurities, and to let your mind develop to its fullest potential. The final level of freedom is what we can call the Tao. In this level of freedom we understand that the whole universe is interconnected, and that we are not isolated individuals. Instead, we're all connected, all together, all one – and in this coming together is the freedom of love and the freedom of seeing what our true path is and how we can grow as people. I accept that this is a rather complicated notion, but it's also a vital one.

What is important for you to know right now is that these two final levels of freedom – the highest levels – both involve a similar process. That process is simple, and I can say that it's the basis of my idea of freedom. It can be summed up in just five words – go towards what you love.

# **Exercise:** *Hierarchy of Freedom*

*Remember Titanic? We don't want you to sink in the process of finding and living your freedom and that's why it's really important that we understand the depth of it before we spend hundreds of thousands of hours pursuing something that we can have instant access to. Most people are striving for the top three of the hierarchy; political, social, and financial. What if you could have access to the purest form of freedom right now, this second?*

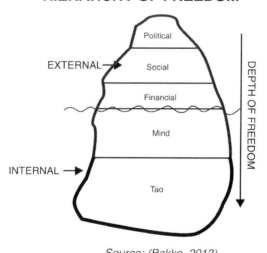

Source: (Bakke, 2013)
www.youwillneverworkagain.com

*Go somewhere out-side where you can sit in peace. I suggest going to a park or somewhere with a bit of nature. Sit on the grass or bench and pick a point in the distance to which you are going to apply some focus, but not too much focus. You should be in-between intense focus and total relaxation. Let´s call this 'soft focus' where you keep your eyes on a single point, but you open up more to your surroundings. Take in the symphony of life around you, feel the wind, sun, rain, warmth or coldness and just take it in while keeping your soft focus on the same point. Stay here until you feel the beautiful symphony of the world around you. This is the Tao, my friend, the ability to see how everything is connected and flowing in perfect harmony.*

*I very much view my business in the same way. I watch and listen attentively and I get great joy in seeing things work naturally, coming and going like the waves of the ocean. This goes for 'bad' things that happen as well as good things. I know that both need to co-exist for the world and my life to be in balance and flow.*

> **Don't forget to watch me explaining this exercise at**
> http://youwillneverworkagain.com/exercises/

This has been quite a philosophical introduction to a book that is, ultimately, about setting up and running your own business. The next chapter, however, starts to get a bit more practical, while still being linked to the same themes as this one. We'll take a look at how you can start gaining some clarity about your true path, and provide some exercises you can try to further define what you want from life.

Don't forget to find out more about freedom, what it means, and how you can make the right steps to grasp it for yourself in my free training videos at http://www.worklessearnmore.tv/.

# Resources

Mark Anastasi, *The Laptop Millionaire: How Anyone Can Escape the 9 to 5 and Make Money Online* (Wiley, 2012) – Anastasi explains how the wealthy people of the world are "we" thinkers, and are rich because they add massive value in the world. Employees are not rich because they typically use "me" thinking, and therefore are more focused on the value they can get. Also a great book for ideas on how to make money online, as well as the core entrepreneurial philosophies.

Timothy Ferriss, *The 4-Hour Work Week: Escape the 9-5, Live Anywhere and Join the New Rich* (Vermilion, 2007) – Ferriss transformed my life when I read his book in 2009. *Never Work Again* should be seen as an answer to what you will be longing for and searching for when reading the *4-Hour Work Week,* as I'll be focusing a lot on what freedom really means to you.

Napoleon Hill, *Outwitting the Devil: The Secret to Freedom and Success*, annotated by Sharon Lechter (Sterling Publishing, 2011) – Not printed until long after his death, this controversial book revolves around Hill's interview with the Devil. He explains how most of society is living in the devil's hypnotic rhythm and are unconsciously carrying out his work without knowing it. By reading this book you will understand more of your deepest desires and why the world works the way it does. Life changing!

Mike Michalowicz , *The Toilet Paper Entrepreneur: The Tell it Like it is Guide to Cleaning up in Business, Even if You are at the End of Your Roll* (Obsidian, 2008) – Powerful and controversial lessons from a serial entrepreneur that has walked the walk. Strongly recommended.

Catherine Ponder, *Millionaires of the Bible Series* (De Vorss & Company, 2000) – Ponder explains that that being wealthy is perfectly compatible with being spiritual, by showing that Abraham, Issac, Jacob, Joseph, Moses and Jesus were not only prosperity teachers, but also millionaires themselves, with more affluent lifestyles than many present day millionaires could conceive of.

Eckhart Tolle, *The Power of Now* (Hodder, 2001) – Tolle shows how to live in the moment to overcome feelings of anxiety and depression while leading a fulfilling life.

Leo Tolstoy, *The Death of Ivan Ilyich* – not exactly the most relaxing piece of fiction you'll ever read, but Tolstoy paints a chilling portrait of a man who realizes his time is up, and regrets the way he has lived his life.

Bronnie Ware, *The Top Five Regrets of the Dying: A Life Transformed by the Dearly Departing* (Hay House, 2012) – A moving example of the final thoughts that go through people's minds, written by a former Australian nurse.

## Software

Omvana Meditation App, containing the guided meditation of "The 3 Most Important Questions" with Vishen Lakhiani, https://itunes.apple.com/us/app/omvana/id595585396?mt=8.

# CHAPTER 3

# Clarity: Finding Your Path

*"Midway this way of life we're bound upon,*

*I woke to find myself in a dark wood,*

*Where the right road was wholly lost and gone."*

~Dante Alighieri, Inferno

# Programming

Are you following your own path in life? You probably think that you are, and that your hopes and dreams come entirely from somewhere within you – but you aren't, and they don't. Don't feel too bad though – practically everyone is, to some degree, following a path that they did not choose themselves, but which was chosen for them. Our desires are not our own, but are programmed into us from a young age – practically from birth – by our parents, our peers, our teachers, and the media. These are the sources of our beliefs about what is the right way to live, what are the things we should be chasing in our lives, how we should behave and act in any particular situation.

This programming creates two major problems for us – it tells us how to work, and it tells us what to want, and in neither case does it do a very good job of considering what is best for us. Let's start with the first of those – how we're programmed to work. Think about when you were at school – what were some of the most important lessons you learned? Apart from the various skills that school is supposed to teach you so that you can get a job working for somebody else, school places a paramount importance on two particular things – you shouldn't copy and you shouldn't get other people to do your work for you. If you copy your art project from Sally and make a few tweaks here and there to improve it, or if you ask Jimmy to write your paper for you in return for letting him borrow your bike, you're going to get in trouble. It's fairly likely that you'll fail your classes if you get caught doing that. And yet, these supposedly terrible acts contain two of the main skills of being an entrepreneur: copying and refining, and leveraging other people's time. Copying and improving on existing ideas and inventions is how innovation happens – which means that copying is the friend of the entrepreneur, who aims to innovate to add value to things that already exist. Leveraging other people's time, meanwhile, is the whole point of this book – if you want to live your life on your own terms rather than being stuck in a cubicle all week, you need to be getting other people to do the work that's going to make you money. I'm going to talk about both of these topics in more detail in a while, so for now let's just make this clear – the mindset you learn in school teaches you to be an employee, and you don't want that, because the world is not set up to benefit employees. The world is set up in such a way that the profits and the free time are both channeled towards the people who own businesses and have other people working for them, while the employees themselves earn less and work more – the opposite of what you want to do.

Think about the mindset that Richard Branson has – he's one of the richest men in the world, a massively successful entrepreneur and businessman, and he dropped out of school at the first possible opportunity, when he was 16. Why has he ended up so successful? It's not because of what he did or didn't learn in school. It's because he has the mindset of an entrepreneur. When you get on a Virgin plane, Richard Branson doesn't check you in; Richard Branson doesn't bring round the snack trolley on a Virgin train; and Richard Branson isn't going to fly people to the moon himself. But what Richard Branson does is leverage other people's time. He comes up with an idea, then he finds people that have the right skills to carry out those ideas for him. That's an entrepreneurial mindset.

The programming we learn in school and from our parents also encourages us to want certain things without really thinking about why we want them. We all end up following roughly the same life path because we believe it is the 'correct' way to go: get educated, get a job, make money, get a promotion, get married, buy a car, get promoted again, make more money, buy a house, have kids, save for retirement, die. The focus is almost entirely on the individual (and perhaps those closest to him, his wife, children, and parents), and individual success is defined in very narrow monetary terms – the more money and material wealth you have, the more successful and secure you and your loved ones will be.

There's a reason why this conception of the 'path of life' is so popular and so common – generally speaking, it works. Throughout human history, it has been a natural and very sensible move to try to accumulate as much as possible during your lifetime, to ensure security for yourself, and to pass your wealth down to your children and grandchildren. This was a very sensible idea during all those centuries in which human beings had less to go around. Even in the past one hundred years, when we have had more luxury than everyone in history before us, this has still seemed like a fairly sensible path – almost anyone can follow it and, unless they are very unlucky or extraordinarily lazy, they can share in the general luxury and wealth of modern times.

But while people who follow this path usually become materially secure, they are often emotionally, intellectually, and spiritually unfulfilled, and subsequently unhappy. Personal growth, health, feelings of enjoyment and fulfillment, social work, friendship, community, education-for-the-sake-of-education – all of these things tend to get lost when we blindly follow the path that is laid out for us. But these things are important too – as we have seen in the previous chapter, without them, we find ourselves to be unhappy and tired, as our grasping, our greediness, and our attachment to the pursuit of money leads us to suffering.

What I am trying to suggest here is that, when it comes to living our life on our own path, there is a difference between 'force' and 'source'. Some things we do, or believe we should do, because of 'force' – because of something external to us, the programming that we learn in school, in the media, and in our families. I'm not trying to suggest that our parents or our teachers literally force us to live our lives in a certain way – but they undoubtedly have a strong influence on us, and encourage us to live our lives in a way that is very similar to most other people. On the other hand, our own opinions, our own true desires, the expressions of our own personality – these come from within us, which is why I call them the 'source'.

You would think that we would listen primarily to the 'source', and only pay attention to the 'force' as a sort of moderation for our wilder instincts. In truth, most of us live our lives following the conventional path dictated to us by 'force' – we follow other people's templates for life, only occasionally listening to our heart, our 'source'. The aim of this chapter is to try and rebalance this relationship – I'm not suggesting you should literally start living out every impulse you have. But, as in the previous chapter, where I suggested that although money is important, there are also things beyond money that are equally important; in this chapter, I am suggesting that while following convention is sometimes useful and necessary, so is finding and following your own true path.

The typical thought when people read this is that they consistently need to "take massive action", or push themselves further and further to differentiate themselves and show their individuality, but that is very dangerous. You do need to push yourself out of your 'comfort zone' and into your 'courage zone' sometimes – that is, you need to stop taking the easiest choice and do something you're a little uncomfortable with, something that scares you a little. Without doing that, you're never going to go anywhere. But if you try to live your entire life in the courage zone, you're soon going to feel overwhelmed  you're going to end up falling into what I call the 'terror zone', where you're continually stressed and worried, and you end up burning out. That's exactly what I used to do, and it ended in a panic attack. You don't want to go down that route.

Instead, you need to find a balance between comfort and courage, and take some time relax, be with yourself, and heal and recharge properly.

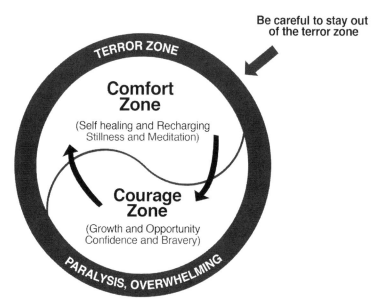

**Be careful to stay out of the terror zone**

TERROR ZONE

**Comfort Zone**

(Self healing and Recharging Stillness and Meditation)

**Courage Zone**

(Growth and Opportunity Confidence and Bravery)

PARALYSIS, OVERWHELMING

*"Everything you THINK you want is just outside your comfort zone, but to live a life of freedom you must find YOUR dynamic between the two."*

*Source: (Bakke, 2013)*

www.youwillneverworkagain.com

A balance is needed between comfort and courage, just like a balance is needed in all things. The famous Taoist symbol of the yin and the yang is important to keep in mind here. The yin and yang represent opposite aspects of our life – some active, courageous, and outgoing, others more reflective and quiet. People often think of those two sides as being opposing forces, but they're absolutely not – they're complementary parts of ourselves, and both sides need the other to balance them out if they are to reach their true fulfillment. The diagram below shows some of these opposite qualities that work together.

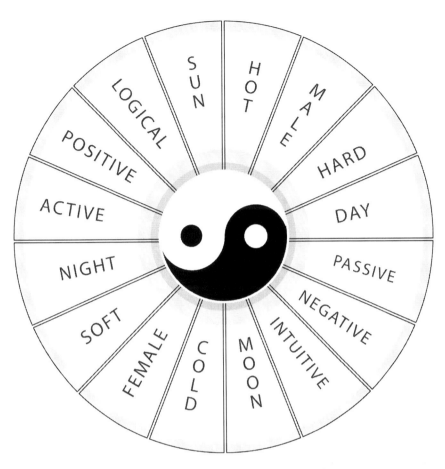

Finding the right balance is often a big problem for entrepreneurs. It's said that around 90% of all entrepreneurs fail within the first five years (although I'm going to discuss in a later chapter why you shouldn't assume that one failure is the end of all your dreams). I would hazard a guess that much of this failure comes about because they don't have the right balance between the abilities they have and the challenges they set for themselves. You can see this on the diagram below. Too many entrepreneurs either challenge themselves too much, more than they are capable of handling with their current abilities, and this leads to burnout. On the other hand, a number of entrepreneurs don't challenge themselves enough – they're talented people, with the ability to go far, but they want to stick to the easy path. Of course, sticking to the easy path is no way to reach the level of success and freedom that you want, and when they don't seem to be going anywhere, they have a problem that we might call 'boreout' – the work isn't interesting enough, they aren't seeing results, so they drop out of the entrepreneurial life.

The most successful entrepreneurs – probably less than 10% of them – are those that can balance their abilities with the challenges they set themselves. They are those who can balance their personal attributes out, working with both the yin and yang sides of their personality. They are those that balance comfort and courage, avoiding the perils of the terror zone. And they are those that balance work with rest, allowing their mind and body to recuperate. Entrepreneurs that can manage this balancing act find themselves in a state of 'flow' – they enjoy their work, and that's the first step to freedom. Crucially, they also know how to get back into the flow if they fall out of it – they take some time out, meet up with friends and family, relax for a little while and allow their batteries (and their creative ideas) to recharge. Later in the book, in chapter six, we'll look at how you can create the good habits that will allow you to maintain this state of flow for a prolonged period of time, avoiding the twin perils of burnout and boreout. And we'll see the habits I apply to stay balanced in my business and to relax as well.

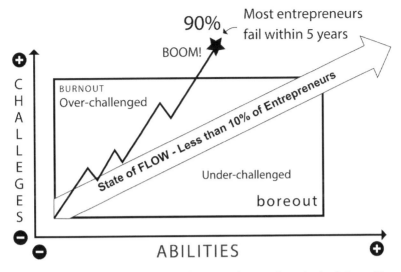

Maintaining a state of flow for a prolonged period of time (5 years +) is the secret to becoming a successful entrepreneur. Create habits that help you avoid burnout so you don't go BOOM!

This chapter aims to help you think calmly and clearly about what your true path is, and how you would live your life if you were also following your 'source' rather than merely copying the ideas of the 'force'. But just before I start giving you some exercises and examples of how to determine what your own path is, I want to elaborate a little more on the idea of 'the path' itself.

## The Eighth Deadly Sin

The programming that we receive from society often seems to be tempting us to act on the seven traditional deadly sins – anger, greed, sloth, pride, lust, envy, and gluttony. In fact, modern marketing techniques are literally designed to appeal to our base desire for those sins – we want to be lazy and to have everything handed to us with no need for work; we want to be greedy and make more money and own more stuff than everyone else; and so on. After all, why do you think I called this book *Never Work*

*Again*? It appeals to greed and it appeals to sloth, and even if you don't think so, you probably have a little bit of both of these within you – there's no shame in it, we're only human after all. And keep in mind that, as we discussed above, all things in life have an opposite side that they balance out with – in this case, the seven sins balance with the seven virtues of kindness, charity, diligence, humility, chastity, forgiveness, and temperance. No doubt you, like the rest of us, have a little bit of the good and the bad within you, and that's fine.

Source: (Bakke, 2013)
www.youwillneverworkagain.com

But I'm not here to moralize to you about the seven deadly sins and traditional morality. Instead, I want to try and redefine the idea of sin a little bit by adding an eighth sin to the list – one which I think is much worse than the occasional indulgence in the other seven (though I encourage you to try to give them up where possible, of course). That eighth sin is when you are missing your mark and not following your path.

The idea that people have a 'path' in life is an easy one for us to grasp, but a difficult one for most of us to implement in our own lives. We've all met people who have known what they want to do for a living, or what their great passion is, from an early age – for example, children who show a great interest in animals and grow up to be vets, or who are very talented at science in school and go on to continue this passion later in life. Things aren't so easy for all of us. We might think of someone who has all the talents and potential needed to be an excellent speaking coach – they have good listening skills, they know how to understand people and provide appropriate advice – but because they follow the more conventional path that schools and society put in front of them, they end up working in something a bit more conventional, like real estate.

From either a religious or secular perspective, we can say that this person is sinning. From a religious perspective, we might say that God gave them all the talent they needed to be a speaker, and they are throwing that away and not following God's will. From a secular perspective, we can say that this person would create more value in the world for other people if they worked as a speaker than they do working in real estate and chasing money. The same goes for you – you'll create more value for yourself and for other people if you're doing something you love, rather than something you simply think will make you money. My good friend Jakob Løvstad, author and founder of Coach Craft, was the one who first told me that the real meaning of sin is 'to miss your mark' – that is, to be off your path – and I think he's right. In Taoism, life is often said to be a river – and going against your path is like swimming upstream. It's much better to go with the flow of life, and to follow where it wants to lead you.

We can take this another level deeper as well. If we assume that our hypothetical real estate worker is sinning, we can also clearly see that they are suffering for their sins. They are, like most people, unhappy and unfulfilled – some estimates suggest that 70% of people are unhappy with their jobs. Perhaps they know they should be doing something else, even if the programming of society hasn't allowed them to work out quite what it should be. This is similar to the idea of *contrapasso* used in Dante's famous poem *The Inferno*, in which one's own sins are the punishment as well as the crime. In this case, the sin is working in real estate rather than following the true path that your talents and interests lead you to. The punishment is...spending your life trading houses and being bored and unfulfilled.

We see the same thing when people take their holidays from work. They spend the entire year anticipating the two or three weeks in which they get to live out their real passions. Why not try to flip this around, and spend a few weeks of the year doing things that feel like work, and the rest of the time enjoying yourself, following your path, being in the 'flow'?

Your true path is unlikely to be involve working a boring job and making more and more money – money is extremely unlikely to be your passion, because despite the advertising industry's successful appeal to our greed and sloth, most people are not naturally that sinful. We do want to own some things and make some money, but very rarely is that the main or only goal in life. And it shouldn't be – after a certain point, you don't necessarily get any happier just because you have more money. In Malcolm Gladwell's recent book *David and Goliath*, he notes that "the scholars who research happiness suggest that more money stops making people happier at a family income of around $75,000 a year". It's the way you live you life and fulfill your path that matters more than your bank balance.

Even when we look at the great entrepreneurs of the past, who make up some of the richest men in history, we see that money was not their motivating factor. Did Bill Gates or Steve Jobs start Microsoft and Apple just to make money? No, they did that work because they loved doing it. Gates and other entrepreneurs and businessmen like George Soros, Andrew Carnegie, and JD Rockerfeller accumulated great amounts of money, and then started giving it away to causes that they thought were more important, like the arts or international development. These people didn't work just for money's sake – they worked for their own passions, and they worked for society by becoming philanthropists. They were not driven by the pettiness of their egos, but by a calling, by what they saw as their path in life. They saw themselves as custodians of wealth rather than possessors of wealth – they were just holding the money until it could be put to the best possible use.

So, if the richest men in the world, who could simply have sat down and waited for more and more money to enter their bank accounts for the rest of their lives, can go through the difficult process of realizing what their true interests and passions are and actively remaining on that path when they could have just relaxed, so can you. It's time to find your own path in life, rather than simply following society's.

## Finding Your Path

We've seen that being on the wrong path is one of the main causes of our suffering and unhappiness – to the extent that we've even called it the eighth deadly sin. But if that's the case, how do we get from the wrong path to the right path? How do we even find out what our true path really is?

The good news is: the path is already inside you. The bad news is: discovering it can be a long and painful process. Tony Robbins argues that the ego is always moving towards pleasure and away from pain as a defensive mechanism – it will always try to take the easiest and most comfortable route, which in this case means sticking with the path that you are already on, the one that society has laid out for us. Going down the more difficult route of examining your life, your desires, and your beliefs is going to feel, to the ego, like you're moving towards pain. The ego is going to be constantly testing you, tempting you into giving up your new, examined lifestyle in favor of going back to the easy route. Make sure you persevere – in the end, you're going to feel much better, be more productive, work less, and be a happier, more fulfilled person, but I must warn you it is a lifelong process. This is not a goal or something you can cross off on a list, but rather an everlasting challenge.

So far I've been filling this book with quotes and ideas from philosophers, religious sages and classic literature, but here's a more down-to-earth example of why you should persevere even when things get difficult. Look at Sylvester Stallone. Now, whether you think his movies are great fun, or unwatchable idiocy, you're probably thinking that of all the people I could have chosen to illustrate this, Sly Stallone seems one of the least likely. But Stallone, as a young man, had a realization of his path. He knew he had within him the idea for a film that was moving, meaningful but also exciting at the same time. So he sat down and wrote the script for it – the script that eventually became the first *Rocky* film – and began trying to sell it around Hollywood. Time and time again he was rejected. This must have been pretty tough for him at the time, a fledgling screenwriter and actor, constantly being told he wasn't good enough. But he knew he had something special, so he kept working on it, refining his script and continuing to show it to anyone and everyone who'd give him the time of day. Of course, as you know, the film eventually got made, was a massive hit, launched Stallone's career and won the Oscar for Best Picture (with Stallone himself nominated for Best Original Screenplay). Say what you like about Sylvester Stallone, but he was right – he did have something special.

You have something special, a medicine for the world, so to speak. You just don't know what it is yet. It might not be an Oscar-winning film, but there is something that you're a natural fit for. Something that your body and mind puts up no resistance against. Something that allows you to feel the flow of true freedom – of being one with the Tao.

I'm going to suggest some ways in which you can start this process of finding your true path. The process starts here, but it doesn't end when you finish reading this chapter, or even this book. In truth, it's a lifelong journey, but as the founder of Taoism Lao Zi said - "a journey of a thousand miles begins with a single step". He was right, and the only way to discover your true path is to start walking it and see where it goes, so consider this chapter the encouragement you need to take the first steps.

## *Exercise:* *Know Thyself*

*Imagine you are the writer of a new film where you will be starring as the main character – yes this film is about you! Everything you truly, deeply want to happen will happen in this film and all the limitations and limiting beliefs you currently have in your life simply do not exist. Imagine you could be, do, and have anything you like and feel great about everything in your life. Write down 7 actions you would take today if you knew you would not fail.*

1. _____
2. _____
3. _____
4. _____
5. _____
6. _____
7. _____

*The point of this exercise is to uncover your deep-hearted desires for the future without the cloudiness of the self-imposed beliefs that have been holding you back from being your true self. Be aware of choosing programmed desires that you 'think' you want, rather than what you truly want deep down. This is a long process that cannot be completed in a 5 minute exercise, but now you have taken the first step on your road of discovery of your true self.*

**Watch me explain this exercise in a free tutorial at**
http://youwillneverworkagain.com/exercises/

## But Why Now?

> *"In the end, people either have excuses or experiences; reasons or results; buts or brilliance. They either have what they wanted or they have a detailed list of all the rational reasons why not."*
>
> ~Anonymous

"I don't want to spend time thinking about all this stuff now, I have a business to build!" Great, I encourage you to get started on that as well – it's another of those journeys of a thousand miles, and you need to take the first step. But it's not an either/or situation – you can start your business and start discovering your path at the same time. And the reason I suggest that you specifically make time to do both of these things is because if you prioritize one of them – and you will almost certainly prioritize business, because it's less painful – you will never find the time to get started on the other. You'll start a business and tell yourself, "I'll just get things started, and once the business is in full swing, then I'll have time to think about this other stuff". You won't, because you never made it a priority – you relegated thinking about freedom and discovering your path, you made it an afterthought, and now it's going to remain an afterthought, because your business is going to start taking up more and more of your time. Because you haven't thought about what freedom really is, and how you need free time to achieve it, you're going to fall into the old trap of chasing after money rather than freedom, and you're going to end up stressed and unhappy, like me at the start of the book.

From this point on, I'm going to be assuming that your path includes being an entrepreneur, but I'll say this one more time before we start – not everyone is cut out to be an entrepreneur or a businessman. Some people are much happier being employees, with all the additional security and lack of risk that entails. There's nothing wrong with that, and it's important that your actions are aligned with your purpose – as we've already seen for example, if you start a photography company when it's not really your calling, you're going to cause yourself a lot of pain until you end up back on the right path. Entrepreneurship's not for everyone – and if it is for you, you'll know.

## Define What Makes You Unhappy

The first step is to 'cut the crap'. There are undoubtedly things in your life that make you unhappy or stressed. Often these are going to be things that you don't really need to be doing, or which are standing in the way of you following your true path because they take up so much time and energy. Maybe you spend five hours a day watching television and then feel bad because you didn't exercise. Maybe you're in a relationship that you're not really happy with, or which is emotionally draining to you. Maybe you're stressed out by all the bills you have to pay each month because you have a big apartment, an expensive car, a hefty phone contract, a cable tv subscription, and so on. Whatever it is that makes you unhappy – define it, write it down, and think about whether you need it. Think about the root causes of the unhappiness – maybe your phone makes you unhappy because you're constantly responding to emails and phone calls and have no free time to yourself. If that's the case, we need to think about ways to reduce that reliance. But maybe the phone itself is fine, and the root cause of your stress is your huge monthly contract – in that case, keep the phone, but switch to something cheaper that still fulfills the things you need or want the phone for.

In life and in business, eliminating things is a recipe for happiness and success. In the cut-throat world of business, when companies cut their staff levels, their stock prices tend to go up – the markets see elimination of costs as a sign of profitability and success. For a more personal example, there's the story of when I moved to San Francisco for a year. I rented out my apartment in Oslo for $2,500 a month. I had to pay $1,500 of that every month to the mortgage company, so that left me with $1,000 a month income – not a lot in a city as expensive as San Francisco. But by living the minimalist lifestyle and hunting for a bargain in the rental market, I ended up actually making money from that deal. I managed to find a place that cost $800 a month, food and wine (yes, wine) included, with a great view of the bay, and I had $200 left over every month that I could save or spend as I choose, even while I was living what would seem to some people like an unattainable dream lifestyle. I proved that it is, in fact, very attainable just by having that minimalist mindset that is focused on the things I really need, rather than constantly chasing after things that I only want. I now make the conscious effort to consume less than I used to – I find myself happier going without things than I was when my life was cluttered with objects and additional costs. If I want something, I rent it for a bit – for example, if I want to try out a new car, I rent it for a while and then give it back, so I'm getting all the benefits of the vehicle, without having to deal with road tax or taking it to the garage for a yearly check up.

## Consider Impermanence

All things are impermanent – why do you think I spent so much time at the beginning of this book discussing death? Everything is impermanent, from your possessions to your life. Thinking about this will help you realize which of these things are truly important to you. When you think about the impermanence of life, you realize that your life could be over tomorrow, for all you know this might be your last 24 hours on earth – so how do you want to live those 24 hours? How are you going to make the most of them? What are the most valuable things you can do with your time?

Thinking about life in this way will help you to 'live in the moment', rather than always focusing on the future and stressing out about accumulating things. Thinking about the impermanence of your possessions will help you to clarify whether you really need to be accumulating more of them – everything you own is eventually going to break down, get replaced, or get stolen, so consider whether the value you get out of those possessions in the meantime is worth their cost. You might think that some of them are worth it, but you might decide that some of them are not – and that the money and time you expend on them could be put to better use in some other way.

## Define What is Important

I expect the answer to be something other than money, by the way. Money is, as I've said earlier in this book, undoubtedly important. Whatever is important to you will probably require you to have some money, because we need money simply to fulfill our basic needs. Maybe what is important to you requires a lot of money – that's fine as well. All I'm trying to encourage here is that you think consciously about what you are making money for, rather than simply making it for the sake of making it. But I also want to encourage you to think about this on as deep a level as you can go – don't just stop at a surface definition of what it is that's important to you – always see if you can ask the question '*why* is this important to me?'. By doing so, you might find that your priorities change and your original answer of what is important to you might not turn out to be the last word at all.

For example, I ask what's important to you, why do you go to work everyday to make more money, what do you want? You say (sounding like a younger version of myself), 'Erlend, my dream is to buy a Porsche'. Great. Absolutely nothing wrong with that, and I wish you the best of luck in one day getting your Porsche. But before you go, *why* do you want a Porsche? Why is a Porsche important to you? Do you actually sincerely desire the particular collection of metal, rubber and engineering that goes to make up a Porsche? Or do you want the status that comes with owning a Porsche? I'm not judging you here, whatever your answer is – it's totally fine for the answer to be that you want the status of being a Porsche owner, that's the same reason I wanted a Porsche. But if that's why you want the car, be honest with yourself, be conscious about your reasons. And then go down another level – *why* is that status important to you? And will the status that comes with owning a Porsche actually fulfill that need within you, or will it require something more? That's a deeper process of questioning which you'll have to face at some point. Maybe you end up deciding that a Porsche is still important to you, and you buy a Porsche one day, and you're very happy with it, and you realize you were right. Absolutely fine, I'm happy for you – but I cannot emphasize enough that you want that process to be one that you have consciously thought about, so that you don't end up buying a Porsche simply because your ego has told you that buying a Porsche is what people do to show everyone else how cool they are. Ninety nine percent of your time (or more) is going to be made up of the process of achieving goals – the actual goal itself only comes at the end of the process, after all – so it is vitally important to ensure that you enjoy the process as well as the goal, otherwise you're going to spend most of your life being miserable.

## *Exercise:* The Gap

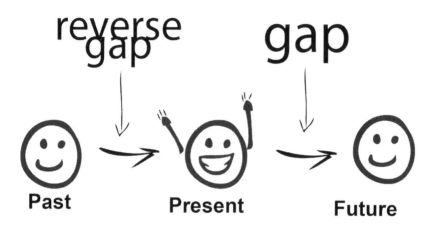

Source: The Revised Gap (Sullivan, 2010)

*This is a mindset technique created by Dan Sullivan. It explains why so many entrepreneurs and people are frustrated. In the middle is who you are right now – ambitious, driven, and motivated. So what you do is create an idea of how you want things to be for yourself in the future; the office space, the cars, the houses and the lifestyle that comes with it, and that's great because that's the way we have been trained to think. That sometime in the future we will be happy. So what we do is delay our happiness in the present and push it into the future. What we start saying to ourselves is that I will do x, y, z when I reach my goals. What tends to happen is when you do realize your goals the joy only lasts for a little blip, before your ambitions, drive, and motivation immediately create another set of high reaching goals that are in the future sometime, and on and on we go. What Dan encourages us to do is to create what he calls "The Reverse Gap" where we remember who we used to be. Where were you 2 years ago?*

*How have you progressed the past 2 years? Have you grown, had experiences, and contributed value in ways you now take for granted? How far have you come and how has your life improved in that time? The importance of this exercise is to understand that you need to focus on both the reverse gap as well as the gap to calibrate your happiness.*

*Write down 5 goals you have achieved the last 2 years that were a struggle for you at the time and acknowledge yourself for those achievements.*

1. _____
2. _____
3. _____
4. _____
5. _____

---

**I talk more about this exercise in one of my tutorials at**
http://youwillneverworkagain.com/exercises/

---

Another example is your family. A lot of people say they want to make more money because they want the best for their family. But too many times they don't take this to the next logical level – *why* do you want the best for your family? Presumably, it's because you love them. And if that's the case, does working a 14 hour day help with that? Or would you be better off maximizing your free time, so that you can actually enjoy what's really important to you – spending time with the people you love? Remember the story about Sam Walton 'blowing it' because he didn't spend enough time with his family? Don't be that guy – make your money, but enjoy your family life as well.

# *Exercise:* The Suitcase

*This is a slightly extreme take on the idea of defining what is important to you, but I think it's good to define the lower limits of what it is is you need to live the life you're aiming for. It's also something that I've actually done for real in the past. When I was first moving from Oslo to London I had to make a quick decision about what to take with me, and I only had one suitcase. I had to very quickly work out what were the absolute most important things to me, the things that I simply had to take with me to London.*

*Try to imagine yourself in the same situation – you need to leave the country in a couple of hours, and you can only take one normal-sized suitcase with you – what do you put in it? What things do you decide to leave behind? Are there things you can simply purchase again when necessary? Are there things that have particular sentimental value that you wouldn't want to leave behind? Whatever they are, they all need to fit into one suitcase. Try not to take more than about thirty minutes to think this through – what you have on your list at the end are the things that are most important to you, the absolute lower limit of what you need and want in your life. You might choose to have more stuff in your life, but at least now you know that if it came down to it, this is all that you need.*

---

**Check out my free video about this exercise at**
http://youwillneverworkagain.com/exercises/

---

# Define What Interests You

In some ways, this is similar to the previous question of what is important to you, but I think it provides a different enough way of thinking about things to be worth a separate entry. I've previously said that the greatest level of freedom is the Tao – the freedom of being at one with the universe, of being part of its 'flow'. I'm going to use another Taoist concept here – that of 'wu wei'. Wu wei literally means 'not doing', but this isn't suggesting you should literally do nothing – but rather, that you should put up no resistance to the natural energy of things. This means different things to different people. Take the example of water flowing over a rock in a stream – the rock and the water are both acting in very different ways, but, crucially, they're both acting naturally. The water is simply being water, the rock is simply being a rock – neither of them has to actively expend any energy to achieve this, they're just doing what they do.

We produce our best work in a state of flow where time and everything else simply disappears and we get immersed in our work on a level that is magical. In other words we become one with the world and just flow with it. We are likely to dip in and out of our flow, which is very natural, but being able to tap into our flow is essential if we are never to work again. Allan Watts explains our life purpose with a metaphor of our life being a river and us being in the river. We may choose whether we want to go with the flow, or swim against the river. Effortless doing will always come when you go with the river of life rather than against it. If there are things in your life that seem unbearably hard to do, you are swimming against the river. This does not mean you should only do things that are easy, that's not the point. The point is to do what comes naturally to you, and be willing to do what it takes to go with your flow.

You should think about your interests in a similar way. There is at least one thing, and maybe more than one, that feels 'natural' to you. Something that you can happily get lost in for hours. Something that, when you're doing it, makes you feel like you've reached that point where you're fully 'in the flow'. These are the best things for you to concentrate on, both in business and in life. As Confucius said all those years ago, "find a job you love, and you'll never work a day in your life". I haven't always followed this advice in my business – my first business was in photography, which it turned out I really didn't love. But eventually I learned my lesson, and I automated and outsourced the business to people who actually love photography. Now I work on the parts of the business that I do love, I'm staying true to my path, and I'm much happier. Even the work I do on my photo business doesn't feel like work anymore because I'm in the 'flow' when I'm doing it, I enjoy it so much. Ideally, having read this book, you'll be able to skip the bits that I did wrong and turn what you love into a profitable business while *also* automating and outsourcing as much of it as possible – and then you really will never work a day in your life.

## Mindfulness: Disconnect from the Intellectual Mind

This is the final entry in the list, but it's actually one of the most important things you can do if you're going to find your path in life – disconnecting from the intellectual mind for a while. Don't worry, we'll be coming back to it – we'll need a bit of intellect and logical thinking when we're helping you set up your new outsourced and automated business. But disconnecting for a while and getting in touch with your more emotional, instinctual, spiritual side can be very rewarding – for one thing, it means abandoning that grasping ego for a while and listening only to your true self, not to your programming. The diagram below shows how your mind is made up of two opposing sources – the Higher Self, which is the source of positive thinking, and the Chatterbox, which is the source of negative thinking and idle gossip. These two sources feed into our conscious mind, which then feeds into our subconscious and determines our actions and feelings. It's impossible (or at least extremely difficult) to fully switch off the Chatterbox, but too many of us leave it on at full volume all the time, drowning out our positive thoughts with distractions and worries. Meditation and mindfulness practices help us to calm down and temporarily silence the Chatterbox, allowing our Higher Self more breathing space and room to explore and grow.

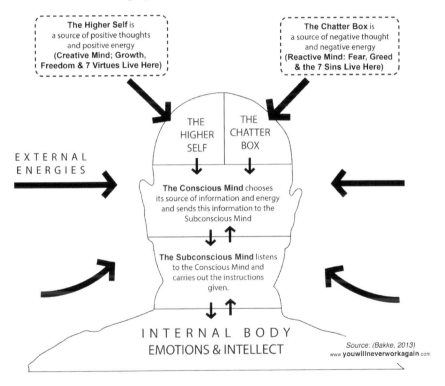

Meditation can also be very useful as a stress reliever. As an entrepreneur you'll be leading a very stressful life, and if something is constantly under pressure it's eventually going to reach breaking point. Meditation gives your mind some space to breathe, so to speak, and by relieving that pressure for just a few minutes you'll be better able to deal with what the day has to throw at you, and your ability for creative thinking and personal growth will be much improved.

I meditate every day, without fail, for thirty minutes, and making this part of my daily routine has been one of the best decisions I ever made – I call it 'the entrepreneur's secret weapon'. You've probably heard all sorts of things about meditation, about people having transcendental experiences with it and so on – and sure, something like that could happen, after a long enough time practicing. But for the beginner, the immediate aim and benefit of meditation is simply to focus on the breath, to quieten the mind, and to sit with yourself for a short time. No distractions, no trying to control things, just stillness.

Meditation and calmness has been shown to make people more effective and better at making decisions as well. In their book *The Power of Full Engagement*, Jim Loehr and Tony Schwartz describe how the world's elite tennis players have a routine that emphasizes calmness and focus inbetween points, which their lesser opponents don't have. The same goes for the elite Formula 1 drivers. This meditative focus, the ability to calm ourselves when trouble or stress arises and to control our emotions and the cries of our ego, allows us to be more effective and productive in our daily lives. Stress generates fear, and fear holds us back – if we can calm our stress by meditating, controlling our breath, and stilling our minds, we can become conscious of our fear and realize that it's really nothing that should hold us back. Instead, as the famous saying goes, we can feel the fear, but do it anyway – we recognize that we have fears, but we can calmly evaluate how reasonable they are, and we don't let them stop us from doing the things we really want to do. Without fear, we make bolder and better decisions, both about our businesses and our lives, which have the potential to lead to greater rewards. That's why I think meditation is a crucial part of really discovering who you are and what your purpose and path is.

While I very much recommend meditation and regularly do it myself, I'm not a meditation teacher, so getting your instructions from me would be a bit of a mistake in this case. In addition, there's a huge range of ways in which you can meditate, and I wouldn't want to force you into following a particular method. However, I have put together a helpful list of more knowledgeable resources that can help you get started on various kinds of meditation, as well as some other Eastern mindfulness practices such as Aikido, Reiki, and Qigong. Head to the resource list at the end of this chapter if you're interested in finding out more.

Ultimately, however you choose to do it, I encourage you to at least try meditating for a while, even if you think this is all airy-fairy hippy stuff – I promise you, the benefits can actually be enormous. As a final example of that – in the first year after I started regularly meditating, my company increased turnover by 50%. The next year, as I got even deeper into my practice, turnover increased by another 85%. It seems that the more I meditate, the more money I make.

# *Exercise:* Meditation

*This is a simple exercise that could have huge benefits for you – quite simply, give meditation a go. The instructions are above, and I also recommend a smartphone application called Mindfulness Meditation (http://www.mentalworkout.com/store/programs/mindfulness-meditation/) when you're starting out. For more detailed information, you can check out the links and references at the end of the chapter. Make some time in your schedule – as little as ten minutes a day – for the next week, and try to sit, be calm, and follow your breath. If you find that it does nothing for you and you're not willing to keep trying, that's fine – but give it at least a week to see how you feel as you adapt to this new experience. And if you do like it – well, keep it up, and even think about slowly increasing the amount of time you meditate for each day. I started at ten minutes, and even now I only do thirty minutes a day – but the benefits are worth so much more.*

> **Find out more about the meditation methods I use at**
> http://youwillneverworkagain.com/exercises/

> *"Praying is asking; meditation is listening"*
>
> ~Anonymous

What I've described above is mindfulness meditation, but that's not the only ancient way to relax your mind and increase your energy. It takes a lot of energy to start a business, and we can get a good idea of how to create this energy by looking at the Chinese idea of 'qi' (pronounced *chee*) – meaning energy, or lifeforce. As well as meditation, there are a number of ancient eastern practices that can help to enhance and refuel your qi. These include reiki (a form of therapeutic massage, a little like acupuncture with the hands instead of needles), aikido (a martial art that focuses on using the force of the attacker against them), and qigong (a series of graceful movements, similar to tai chi, designed to allow the free movement of qi throughout the body). Some of you might be a little skeptical about these kinds of practice, but I promise you that if you give any of them a go (and there will be classes for them in almost any major city of the world), you'll soon find yourself feeling much healthier, more relaxed, and less tired. Aligning your qi through these practices can make you a better entrepreneur by helping you to avoid the curse of many new businessmen – burnout and exhaustion.

## The Purpose of Defining Your Path

We're about to be moving on to the more practical side of the book, and those of you who have read through everything so far might be wondering why we didn't just start there. Why all this talk of freedom, death, and paths? Well, there's a good reason why I've focused on this first – by thinking about these issues, you're also going to develop a better understanding of some of the things I'm going to discuss in the second half of the book. At this point, you will hopefully have started to understand what makes you happy in life, what you enjoy working on, and what you consider truly important. Now, if you ask yourself 'what do I need to make this happen?', most of the answers are likely to fall into two major categories – *time* and *money*.

And that's what the rest of the book is going to be about – how to create more time and money for yourself through your business. There's a lot of business books already out there that will help you to make more money – although I think that this book complements them and gives you the information you need to run a really effective business with very little investment. But there's not that many books that focus on time. I think this is a mistake, and the reason why Tim Ferriss' *The 4-Hour Work Week*, which does focus on time as well as money, is so popular. Money you can always make more of, you always have another chance; time is finite, once it's gone, it's not coming back. Whatever you're starting to realize through reading this chapter and completing the exercises, whatever you think your true path or your real priorities are, they are going to require time. And that's what I want to show you in the rest of this book – how to best use the most precious commodity on earth: time.

Ultimately, I want to change the way you think about your goals. I want you to focus less on the final achievement of the goals that you set for yourself, and more on the process of moving towards those goals. Yes, the achievement is important and enjoyable, but if you spend the years beforehand suffering and being miserable, is it really worth it? Especially when you can set yourself up to achieve goals while also enjoying the day-to-day progress towards them. What I'm trying to suggest is that living and being happy *now* is as important as achieving your long-term goals – and if you let your goals become your obsession, then living for the moment becomes impossible, and you will always delay your happiness in favor of that future goal. Don't do it. All you'll find is that when you start to get near to achieving the goal, you'll become disappointed. Achieving the goal doesn't provide you with the massive burst of everlasting happiness that you were banking on. So you end up setting yourself a new goal to take its place, one even further in the future, one that will *definitely* be the thing that makes you happy. And so the cycle begins again.

Instead, have goals, but also have an understanding that you need to be happy and fulfilled on a daily basis. The less you orient every facet of your life around your goals, the less you focus on some ultimate idea of what will make you happy, and the less ego-driven you are in your thoughts and actions, the more successful you will tend to be – this has always been the case for me. Strange as it sounds, once you really stop craving things and chasing after the desires of your ego, suddenly those things come to you much easier than they did before.

## A Final Wake Up Call

To finish off this section of the book, I want to give you a few little statistics. I worked this out once while I was waiting for a flight at London City Airport. As the seconds, minutes, and hours ticked past on the clock, I started thinking a lot about time and its endless movement, and I started adding things up and measuring them.

I thought to myself, how many days is there in a human life? Three hundred and sixty five days, multiplied by, let's say, eighty years. That's 31,025 days. Sounds like a lot, but then remember that by the time you reach the age of thirty, you've already been alive for 10,950 of them. That gives you just over 20,000 days left. In hours, that's twenty four times twenty thousand – 480,000 hours left. Great, still sounds like quite a lot, I can get back to watching the television. But – you're asleep for roughly one-third of that – so now you're down to about 320,000. Maybe you spend half an hour a day having a shower, brushing your teeth and getting dressed – and I know some of you will probably take longer than that – that's another 10,000 hours gone. Maybe two hours a day buying, preparing and eating food? Another 40,000 hours. If you have a job, it gets even worse – thirty-five more years of work until you can retire. Two hours in a car on all those days – over 25,000 hours. Eight hours at work on all of those days – 102,200 hours. Just adding all of those numbers up, you're down to just over 140,000 hours of free time left in your entire life from the age of thirty onwards. That's 5,950 days. That's 16 years. So, following the conventional path of life from the age of thirty onwards, you're going to be alive for another 55 years, and only 16 of those are yours to do what you want with. There's a great little video about this by the artist Ze Frank at http://youtu.be/BOksW_NabEk.

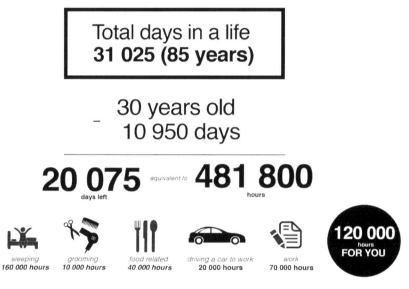

Source: (Bakke, 2013)
www.youwillneverworkagain.com

I have three points here:

- The first is that you don't have much time left, when you really think about it, so start now. Even small actions towards improving your life and making yourself happier will have an impact. Even slow progress is progress, so start doing something that counts (reading this book and doing the exercises is a good way to begin, I should note).

- The second point is that you should try to avoid following that conventional path of getting a job, and should instead be an entrepreneur and an owner of your own business – that way, you can start to cut out some of those things that are stealing time from you, like the commute to work and the eight hour work day itself.

- My third point is that you can create even more time for yourself without having to sacrifice making money – by creating efficient business systems that take advantage of techniques of automation and outsourcing.

Which chapter to read next depends, to some extent, on where you are in your development as a businessman or entrepreneur. If you already own a business that is running reasonably smoothly, but which you would like to take up less of your time and effort, then you may feel able to skip the next chapter and go straight to chapter five, where we start discussing the techniques of how to work less and earn more. If you're new to running a business, or you haven't gotten started yet, I recommend reading the next chapter to give yourself some ideas and inspiration about how to get going. In general, the rest of the chapters in this book are all really about one thing – taking something you love doing, and leveraging other people's time to build a business that makes money and lets you enjoy life to the fullest. Building systems that use other people's time for your benefit is the main business skill you'll need to ensure you can work on your passions and follow your path without going broke in the process.

Looking for more information about how to find your true path, understand your desires, and take your first steps towards freedom? Then try my free video training at http://www.work lessearnmore.tv/.

# Resources

Andrew Carnegie, *The Autobiography of Andrew Carnegie* – the self-written story of a remarkable man. It's always a good idea to see how the masters do it, and Andrew Carnegie was nothing if not a master of entrepreneurship.

Doc Childre, Howard Martin & Donna Beech, *The Heartmath Solution: The Institute of HeartMath's Revolutionary Program for Engaging the Power of the Heart's Intelligence* (Harper Collins, 2000)

Benjamin Franklin, *The Autobiography of Benjamin Franklin* (P.F. Collier, 1909)

Carl L. Gould, *The 7 Stages of Small Business Success* (Keynote, 2010) – A great book on understanding the importance of small business success, with special emphasis on understanding how to build teams and knowing thyself through the well known DISC system.

Jakob Løvstad, *The Arts Volume 1: A Strange and Mysterious Journey* – written by a good friend of mine, this is the best book I know on how to discover and follow your own path.

Geshe Michael Roach and Lama Christine McNally, *The Diamond Cutter: The Buddha on Managing your Business and Your Life* (Doubleday, 2009)

Richard Strozzi-Heckler, *In Search of the Warrior Spirit: Teaching Awareness Disciplines to the Military* (Blue Snake Books, 1990)

DT Suzuki, *An Introduction to Zen Buddhism* (Grove Press, 1994) – probably the best theoretical introduction to Zen Buddhism and meditation available – again, Suzuki was a master on his subject, and one of the best people to learn from.

A. Westbrook & O. Ratti, *Aikido and the Dynamic Sphere* (Tuttle Publishing, 1970)

# Some Mindfulness Links

Wildmind Buddhist Meditation

(http://www.wildmind.org/) - a very clear, well thought-out website with a huge number of tutorials on how to meditate effectively. Take your time to explore the site and clarify anything that's causing you problems.

Mindfulness Mediation by Mental Workout Inc., $1.99 through the iTunes Store - I love this app and always recommend it to people that are interested in gaining the benefits of doing daily meditations.

Pranayama - Health Through Breath by Saagara, $5.88 through the iTunes Store - This is the app I use every single morning before starting my day. Pranayama is a very powerful meditation and I strongly suggest you start at the lowest level of the app and gradually work yourself upwards as you get more conditioned to the exercise. Check with your doctor before using it if you have any illnesses because people have fainted while doing these exercises and I must warn you it's quite addictive when you get started.

Infinite Relaxation by Michael Schneider, $3.99 through the iTunes Store - Fantastic app to use before going to bed instead of watching tv. Makes you sleep like a peaceful baby.

Deep Sleep with Andrew Johnson by Michael Schneider, $1.99 through the iTunes Store - I fall asleep to this app a couple of times a week. I have used it for more than 3 years and all I have to do when I'm feeling stressed before bed is put it on and I flow into sleep within 5-10 minutes. Love it!

Abraham Hicks Vortex Attraction Guided Meditations by Abraham Hicks Publications, $14.99 - This app is all about flow and allowing the universe to provide for you through your thinking. I enjoy the abundance soundtrack which makes me shift from thinking about what I don't have to what I do have, and that we do live in a world full of abundance if we are open to receiving it. You have to take action for this to work!

Insight Timer - Meditation Timer by Spotlight Six Software - When doing Reiki you place your hands on different parts of your body as part of the meditation exercise. You should attend a Reiki course before you start doing this form of meditation so you get good guidance and open up your body for this art of self-replenishment. You can find endless amounts of playlists on Reiki on music services such as Spotify. I suggest making your own playlist that works best for you.

Modern QiGong by Lee Holden, $99 produced by MindValley - You can start doing Qigong without any prior skill or knowledge of the practice. You stream the session on your laptop and just follow what Lee tells you to do. I have done these exercises with people aged from 10 to 90 and it's an amazing experience! Feeling stressed and tired? Qigong does wonders for getting more energy and just generally feeling super amazing. It's difficult to explain before you try it.

Aikido – There are many videos of Aikido on YouTube. Here is a nice demonstration of the martial art that I have chosen to practice: http://www.youtube.com/watch?v=aicHsMC6rxM

# CHAPTER 4

# Your Freedom Business

*"Do you own a system or a job?...
The reality is that there are unlimited
new ideas, billions of people with
products and services to offer, and only
a few people who know how to build an
excellent business system."*

~Robert Kiyosaki, Cashflow Quadrant

# Modeling

To open this chapter, I want to address one thing that often troubles new entrepreneurs. This is going to involve saying something that sounds controversial, so I'll get straight to it – copying is a good thing. I'm not talking about outright plagiarism, and copyright infringement isn't going to help you as a budding entrepreneur, but copying at a more general level is not only a good thing – it's a vital part of the way innovation occurs. You may remember that the first business I started on my own was a carbon copy of what I had already done, because I knew how to make that business happen. I asked my old business partner for an 'ok' before I did this. Of course, as we've seen, I knew deep down that photography was not for me, but I did it anyway.

If you read the book *Borrowing Brilliance* by David Kord Murray, you'll see what I mean. Basically, everything is interdependent, and nothing is completely original. Every new product or invention is built on a backbone of the inventions and products that came before it. Even a company like Apple, who are usually thought of as being unusually innovate and imaginative, are primarily building their innovation and imagination on top of pre-existing technologies, marketing strategies and business systems. Then they test them, they measure them, and they refine them until they are so much better than the originals that we hardly even recognize them as the same thing. But they are, ultimately, doing the same as everyone else – they're just doing it better.

There's two things you can learn from this. The first, is that you shouldn't be afraid to borrow. Say you want to start a food business (it's not one of the recommended models I'm going to talk about in this chapter, but maybe you're really passionate about food, you know it's your true calling in life, and you're confident you can do it). When you're setting up your business system, why start from scratch and re-imagine every little detail from nothing? Instead, study how existing successful businesses do their work, and build on their system. Let's say you want to start a business selling healthy fast food, because you think it's terrible that so many people go to McDonalds. You might think to yourself that you want nothing to do with the golden arches, that you want everything in your business to be the opposite of what McDonalds stands for and does. In actual fact, you'd be much better off if you took McDonalds as the starting point for your business, because whether you like it or not, they have spent several decades creating an incredibly efficient business system that allows them to sell food cheaply and attract millions of customers every day. By all means, sell food that is the complete opposite of a Big Mac and fries; but don't assume that you're above the McDonalds business model. If you're going to sell fast food, it's the model you should be starting with and building on.

The second lesson is, don't be afraid to share. A problem that many entrepreneurs have at the beginning of their careers is paranoia. They think, "I have a brilliant, world-changing idea...and I can't tell anyone until it's a completely finished product, because someone will steal it". Of course, your idea is not going to get very far if people don't hear about it. Your idea will have more chance of being successful if you make connections, tell people about it, make people enthusiastic for it – in general, if you send it out into the world. Think of it as being part of the entrepreneur mindset – your idea should be adding value to the world, and therefore the more people know about it, the more people will want to pay you for it. If it's only in your head and you guard it obsessively, it's not creating value for anyone.

Over time, if your idea is successful, other entrepreneurs will start building on your system and your ideas for their own projects. That's fine – you already built on someone else's work for your successful project, now these people get to do the same with yours. They might refine it and take it new directions that you'd never have thought of, and that's also fine. At the same time, you are constantly testing and refining your own systems, so you're also building in different directions. And both you and the other people who build on your system are all creating more value in the world and providing products and services that people want. None of this is a problem – it's just how the process of innovation works.

## No Money Down Business Blueprints

With that in mind, this is where things start to get real. We've talked about philosophy and how to start understanding your true path. Now it's time to start talking about business, and the models that you can borrow from to start your own company. This chapter is written as a primer for anyone who has yet to start their own business, and is looking for a way to test the waters without having to commit to a massive investment. I don't believe business should be restricted to those who have thousands of dollars to invest right from the beginning, but luckily, in our digital age, it doesn't have to be. I own three businesses, and none of them have required a large amount of money upfront – the advantage of this 'no money down' model is that it gave me the freedom to experiment, to make mistakes, and, most importantly, to learn and to not be afraid of starting again. If you're investing your life savings into a business, you're going to be cautious, careful, safe. If you're spending no more than a few hundred dollars on a website or some phone calls to other businesses, you can afford to be risky and try out new things – if it goes wrong, you're not going to miss a couple of hundred; if it goes right you could be making ten times that every month – and much more.

# *Exercise:* Love Money

*Now that you know what you love and want in life it's time to build a business that allows you to make money on just that. When it comes to a freedom business, you must try to create a product of some sort to sell or scale up your value in some shape or form. If you love yoga then create an instructional video on how to do Yoga. The important element of a freedom business is having a scalable product and having other people deliver it for you through employment or outsourcing.*

*Write down what you love doing on a piece of paper and you will see how you can make money on it throughout this chapter.*

> **I talk more about this issue in one of my free tutorials at**
> http://youwillneverworkagain.com/exercises/

Now, if you're thinking about starting a business, the most important thing you need to know is that a business is a system. It's a set of inputs, processes and outcomes which can be repeated over and over again. This means that, while a business undoubtedly has a large element of trial and error, of trying things over and over again in slightly different combinations until they work the way you want, the basic elements of a businesses can be planned out in advance. The other great advantage of developing a well-planned business system is this: if you're doing it right, you do not need to be part of the system. The inputs to the system can be other people

– your outsourced employees – who perform the processes and achieve the results, with the majority of the benefits going to the owner of the system, which is you. Your own role becomes nothing more than overseeing the system, while leveraging other people's time to actually operate it.

This is what this chapter is all about. As part of my company Mr Outsource (http://www.mroutsource.com/), which is a recruitment company for entrepreneurs that want to start outsourcing, I've developed a number of 'blueprints' for business models that are most conducive to this kind of work, as well as gathering case studies and interviews from leading experts in these industries, and I'm going to share them with you here. These blueprints correspond to the kinds of business that are most suited to the techniques of outsourcing and automation that I'm going to explain in future chapters – they are business models that will make you money while giving you the spare time to pursue your own passions and desires. But the best bit of all? They are NO MONEY DOWN freedom business blueprints – they all require no investment, or extremely minimal investment (for example, paying for a website), meaning you can experiment with them, test them, and refine them without worrying about your money disappearing. The 'blueprint' aspect also means they're perfect for the outsourcing and automation techniques I'm going to discuss in later chapters, because they're already built around pre-planned systems. Systems in which you leverage other people's time are the most important thing in building effective businesses, because they make things easier for you, they mean the business will continue to work and to make money even when you're taking a holiday on a tropical island somewhere, and they mean you can eventually sell the business for large amounts of money because investors know that it will work even when you're gone (this is the basic principle of John Warrillow's book *Built to Sell*). Ultimately, you start a business to eventually sell a business, so that the value you've created can carry on growing, even if you are not there.

> *"The entrepreneur creates an enterprise,*
> *the technician creates a job."*
>
> ~Michael E. Gerber

I'm going to show you some examples of business blueprints I've used in the past, and also talk to a few other people who have been successful in these businesses and have some useful words of advice for those who are just starting out. This section is quite long, but don't feel like you have to read every word. Just check out the PDF files of the blueprints that I'm going to link to, read the first few paragraphs of each section where I give you a quick run down of how the business works, and then, if it's for you, read on – if not, feel free to move on to the next blueprint until you find one that appeals.

## How the Blueprints Work

A business blueprint is split into nine sections which need to be filled in. In the examples below, adapted from Osterwalder's business model canvas, I've filled those spaces in for you. I have also written a detailed explanation of each blueprint, which you can read by clicking on the relevant links in each section. If you're thinking of starting a different kind of business, these are still things you'll need to think about and fill in beforehand – there's a blank canvas coming up in a few pages for you to look at. The nine areas are:

- Key partners – no man is an island, and if you're going to do business, you're going to need to work with reliable partners at some point.

- <u>Key activities</u> – what are the main activities you will be undertaking as part of this business? This doesn't just include the customer-facing activities (i.e. selling things to people), but also the main activities you'll need to be doing before you get to that stage (i.e. finding the right products, marketing, etc.).

- <u>Key resources</u> – what resources do you need in order to succeed with your key activities? What are the things you simply won't be able to do without if your business is going to succeed?

- <u>Value proposition</u> – as far as your potential customers are concerned, what do you bring to the table? What do you offer that makes you stand out in the marketplace? What are your primary selling points, the things you are going to market yourself on?

- <u>Customer relationships</u> – what kind of relationship are you going to have with your customers? Are you looking to create a trusted but occasional relationship with them, so that when they want a specific kind of product they think of you? Are you entering a niche market, so that your customers have to come to you because of a lack of other options? Do you want devoted fans who will come to you no matter what, like Apple?

- <u>Customer segments</u> – who is your audience? What particular groups of people are you trying to target?

- <u>Channels</u> – what channels are you using to market and sell your products? In many cases, these will be entirely digital and internet-based, but for some other businesses with different target audiences, there may be different channels for your product.

- <u>Cost structure</u> – where are you going to be spending money? Carefully plan the main sources of your expenditure, so things don't take you by surprise later on.

- <u>Revenue streams</u> – equally important, where is your profit coming from, or where do you expect it to come from? If you don't have an answer to this, you don't have a business.

On the final two points – that of revenue and costs – I want to emphasize before we go any further that as much as 60% of your costs should be going on sales and marketing. Those are the things that create future revenue for you. If production and operations costs come to more than 40% of your spending combined, you need to re-evaluate your model or recalibrate your spending. That's why a lot of the business models in this section have an emphasis on marketing and driving internet traffic to your business – because that's where the majority of your costs should be. Take a look at the diagram below for inspiration.

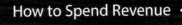

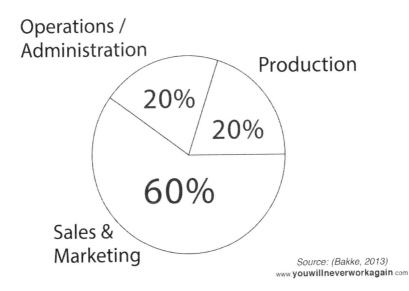

Source: (Bakke, 2013)
www.youwillneverworkagain.com

These nine areas apply to any business you might be thinking of starting – once you've thought them through in detail, you'll be well prepared to get going. Now I'm going to discuss some of the business models I've used in the past in more detail – including filling out those nine areas for you, and discussing the pros and cons of each model. You don't have to follow the same route as me – but these are tried and tested, no money down models for successful businesses.

> *"It does not matter how slowly you go*
> *as long as you do not stop."*
>
> ~Confucius

Oh, and one final thing before we take a look at the blueprints – while all of these business models require no money down and offer the chance for you to build a freedom business, the early stage of all of the models requires one very important ingredient – perseverance. That means that even if things seem a little tough at the beginning, you need to stick them out. Don't deviate from your path if things get difficult – stay true to yourself and your purpose in life, and things will naturally click into place sooner rather than later.

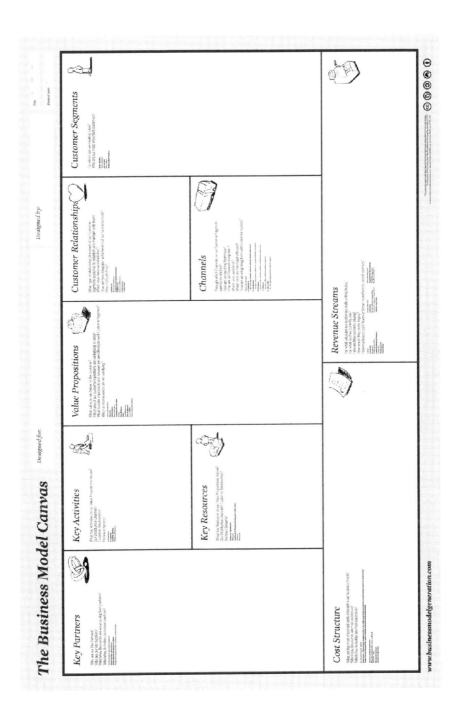

# Dropshipping

The first business blueprint is for dropshipping. In its essence, dropshipping means working together with a company that produces desirable products to market and sell those products. You need to find wholesalers who are looking for this kind of relationship (one of the more difficult parts of this model, admittedly), and create a website on which you will advertise the product in question and offer potential customers the option to buy it. When a customer places an order, the details are sent to the manufacturer of the product, and they ship it to the customer, usually with labels referring to the name of your company. The trick, of course, is that on your website you are charging more than the wholesaler charges – and the difference between the two prices is your profit.

1 You market our products to your customers

2 Your customer orders the product from you

3 You charge the customer a price that works for you

6 Your customer gets the order with YOUR company info

5 We ship the order to your customer and email you the tracking numbers

4 You place the order with us and we dropship the item

*Source: (Bakke, 2013)*
www.**youwillneverworkagain**.com

Here's an example from my own work – our YouSpin store (http://youspin.myshopify.com). I found a supplier of photography equipment through the ecommerce site Alibaba (http://www.alibaba.com/), and got in touch with them. I set up the shop through Shopify (https://www.shopify.com/), which handles all the technical aspects of this kind of thing for $30 a month. Now, when I get an order, one of my staff in the Philippines takes care of the whole thing – he accesses the system, coordinates the delivery with the supplier, and bundles it all together into a little report for me at the end of each month, detailing all the transactions made. This has been going on for about a year now, and I make around $2000 a month from it. Doesn't sound like a huge amount? Maybe not, but this is the important part – that $2000 comes from 30 minutes of work on my part. That's 30 minutes every month. Essentially, that's $4000 an hour. All because I set up a system that works, and that works without me needing to do anything other than keep my eye on it once a month, for half an hour – the rest of the work that the business needs to keep going is done on other people's time.

---

### See the Dropshipping Business Blueprint at
www.youwillneverworkagain.com/bonus

---

The advantages of this model are that it has a low startup cost and does not require you to store a large inventory of products – you're simply acting as a a middleman for the vendors, leaving the cost of storage on them. In turn, they benefit from the fact that you are focusing on sales and marketing of their products, so they can spend less in those areas. Other advantages are that this is very easily outsourceable, and can be done entirely online from a laptop with an internet connection, allowing you to travel and live a location-independent lifestyle. You can experiment with a wide range of products, either on the same site or on a number of different sites, allowing you to take advantage of multiple opportunities. The disadvantages are that it's a very competitive market, and to really make yourself visible, you'll find that you eventually have to start spending more on marketing costs.

Hopefully, this will be offset by your increased profits, but it is a risk, and it's a risk that you'll have to take eventually if you're going to break big in this industry.

Some final tips that I have on dropshipping businesses – you need to really do a lot of research and planning before fully jumping into this one, to ensure you have reliable partners and high quality products. You're going to need to negotiate well with potential partners, and really think through every possible scenario to make sure you're going to be maintaining a profit margin on each item sold. You also need to negotiate, in writing, a returns policy with the wholesaler – you don't want to be taking on the cost of the item every time a customer is unhappy. Remember that the customer is king in a business like this, and providing excellent customer service should not be an afterthought, or a thing you tack on at the last moment – it should be a necessity and it should be in your plans from the very beginning. Finally, when thinking about products to sell, try to focus on niches or on particularly rare and expensive items, rather than common things. Every niche has an audience, and capturing the relatively small audience for that niche is easier and requires less marketing than trying to make yourself visible in a crowded marketplace for a very common product. Equally, while higher price items may be harder to sell, you'll make more money on each sale, and you'll usually need less customer service for these less common, more expensive items. However, the case study below will show that this may be the easiest freedom business you can start today.

## How to Make $25,000 a Month From Dropshipping

Wanting to find out a little bit more about how other entrepreneurs use dropshipping to build their own freedom, I got in touch with a good friend of mine, Bishop Stewart. It turns out, his method of dropshipping is even simpler than the one I use. "When I started out, I was trying all sorts of different approaches to making money online," Bishop told me over the phone from Los Angeles. "but none of them were really working for me. They all required too much overhead, too many fixed costs, which I was trying to avoid. And then one day a friend of mine introduced me to the idea of dropshipping and put me in touch with another of his friends who had made millions of dollars doing it. From that point on, the simplicity of it had me hooked, really."

"The beautiful thing about drop shipping is that it doesn't require a website or a big existing mailing list – it takes literally seconds to set up because you're leveraging the infrastructure and the credibility of existing websites. In my case, I find products that are available on Amazon, and list them on eBay at a higher price with eye-catching pictures and snappy, keyword-filled headlines. When someone orders and pays through eBay, I order from Amazon and enter their shipping details – the difference between the Amazon price and the price I listed on eBay is my profit."

At this point, I had to ask: don't people get annoyed when the box turns up with an Amazon logo and an invoice that references the lower price that you paid? It seems not - "I worried about that as well in the beginning, but really, people just want the thing they ordered, they don't question exactly where it comes from. I've had one or two people ask me about it, and I tell them that I ran out of stock and ordered it from Amazon as a courtesy to make sure they got their product."

Bishop has since branched out from simply using Amazon, and now makes as much as $24,000 profit in a single month by selling big ticket items with larger profit margins. "CostCo, for example – they have a lot of great stuff at very low prices, and they ship for free. At times, I've made $200 or $300 profit on some of their items."

"It was originally taking me around four to five hours a day," Bishop continues, "because when you start out and you're learning the ropes it can take a while to list things. Today, it takes me around two and a half hours a week, because I've outsourced most of the work to a virtual assistant (VA) in the Philippines. She lists the items, sends the orders, and sends me a spreadsheet telling me what we've sold and what the profit is. She also checks that the prices and items are still available on the websites we're using – this is very important, because in the beginning we had a few problems with items going out of stock on Amazon without us noticing. Telling a buyer you can't give them the product they ordered is a surefire way to get negative feedback, which you want to avoid at all costs – that's also why I accept returns, because you lose a lot of credibility on eBay if you don't. You can usually send the item back to Amazon yourself when it reaches you, so you don't have to lose out."

Any final tips for someone thinking about starting out in dropshipping? "Sure – avoid electronics, iPhones, and 'as seen on tv' products, because those companies get scared that you're sending out cheap knock-offs, and they'll write to you asking you to take the listings down. Make sure you specify that you don't ship internationally, or to any of the places that Amazon won't deliver to – Hawaii, Alaska, PO Boxes, military addresses, and so on. And apart from that, just focus on your keywords and on getting inside the mind of your customers and what they are searching for – for instance, 'chair' is too generic, you need to use words like 'ottoman', 'upholstered', 'accent', words that people are searching for to find the specific chair they want."

## Freedom Business Fact File

**Name:** Bishop Stewart
**Location:** Los Angeles

**Where will you be in 5 years?:** I intend to double my business each year, which should put me on about $500k in a few year's time. But then, if I can get there, why not a million?

**Where can we find out more?:** Head to my website, http://www.bishopstewart.com/, or you can send me an email at bishop@bishopstewart.com – put 'dropshipping training' in the subject line, so I know what it's about.

When telling me about his website, Bishop mentioned he was working on it with a woman he met at a conference – Carmena Su, who at the time was struggling with her own attempts to make money online. Since starting to dropship five months ago, Bishop said, she was now making $10,000 a month profit – amazingly quick progress. I figured Carmena would have a few lessons for any budding dropshippers reading this book, so I reached out to her as well. Her story was similar to that of many online entrepreneurs – after an offline business failed in the crash of 2009, she tried out various things online before discovering the thing that worked for her – dropshipping.

"I didn't really understand it at first," Carmena told me, "and I thought I would be handling the products, which didn't really appeal – but once I got it, I tried listing something small to see how it worked. I found a frying pan on Amazon and listed it on eBay, and was surprised to see that it sold – it wasn't even the cheapest one on there! It's really such a simple system – essentially, you're just shopping for deals, but instead of actually buying things you act as the middleman for other people, collecting a margin when the item sells. That's it."

The thought of immediately going to eBay and listing sofas and other items with profit margins in the hundreds of dollars was appealing to me more and more. But Carmena sounded a note of caution - "you have a dollar limit on how much you can sell when you first start in eBay, so it helps to stick to multiple small items first to build up your positive feedback. At that point, you can ring eBay, point to your good reputation, and ask them to raise the limit – which they're usually very happy to do, since they make a commission from each item sold."

Since her success on Ebay, Carmena has found even greater success as a seller on Amazon.com. "It blows my mind how much you can sell on Amazon as visitors there have only one intention: to buy something. If you can master the art of sourcing products, you can take advantage of price discrepancies and list on Amazon all day. There are no seller limits which is great."

Like Bishop, Carmena outsources much of the work to a VA. "I had a problem where I was selling so many things that my source went out of stock without me noticing – and you can get your account put under review when you fail to deliver what you promise. I had an outsourced worker on one of my other businesses at the time, so I decided to move them over to this one to avoid that happening again. They check the stock and the prices and relist items for me – the only thing I don't recommend outsourcing is the titling of the items. That's very important, and unless you're working with a native English speaker it's too easy to get it wrong."

Carmena told me that the main skill needed is simply perseverance and the ability to not get too caught up in the details. "People can sometimes have the 'paralysis of analysis', where you spend all your time worrying about why one item isn't selling, or wondering how another seller can afford to list things at a lower price. Don't get obsessive like that, just focus on the bigger picture – there are millions of products in the world, so find something else. And never stop believing that you can do it if success doesn't happen right away. Understand what you're doing, master it so you can show someone else what to do, then outsource the parts you don't enjoy."

## Freedom Business Fact File

**Name:** Carmena Su
**Location:** New Zealand

**Where will you be in 5 years?:** Turning over high six figures, if not seven figures and showing others how to do the same. I love this business model because it puts the power of billion dollar corporations in your hands. There is no limit to what you can do.

**Software:** Basecamp, for dealing with my outsourcers; Google Docs; and the software that I use to track price changes on Amazon.com.

**Where can we find out more?:** If you're reading this and you're new to online businesses or you've yet to have success, I encourage you to email me at carmena@ytcfilms.com, and put 'NWA Dropshipping in the subject line. You can also check out the website that Bishop and myself have teamed up on, http://www.bishopstewart.com/.

---

**To hear the full interviews with Bishop and Carmena, go to**
http://www.youwillneverworkagain.com/experts/

---

## Information Marketing

Information marketing is exactly what it sounds like – the product you are marketing is information. This can be in the form of ebooks, podcasts, webinars, in-person seminars and training sessions, or any other format you can think of in which you take knowledge that you have and that other people want, and transmit that value at a cost. The main difference between this kind of business and the others I'm discussing is that, in information marketing, you can brand and sell yourself – for example, by marketing yourself as an expert on a particular topic via a blog or personal website – or you can find and sell someone else's information product. The latter is easier to do, but you'll have no control over the product. This can be quite a difficult business model to start making a profit in, due to the need to build a strong relationship with a customer base *before* they spend much money, but once you create that relationship the rewards can be great.

One important idea in this branch of work is the 'sales funnel' – the idea that you are always trying to funnel customers towards a more expensive product. So you start by giving things away for free – blog posts, for example. These blogs begin to establish you as an expert in your chosen field and you can start to sell more in-depth writing in the form of books. This increases your credibility and your audience, and you can sell webinars and seminars at which you discuss things in even more detail and train small groups of people. The final aim is usually to sell one-on-one coaching or mastermind groups in your chosen topic, the most expensive and lucrative option for an information marketer.

This book itself is an example of an information marketing product. You paid for this book because of the information it contains and the value that information holds to you. And on my side, I hope that through reading it you'll be convinced to sign up for one of my webinars, seminars, or maybe check out my podcast at www.hardcoremba.com. You can check out all the products that I offer in the marketing funnel diagram below.

## Erlend´s Information Marketing Funnel

**Free Stuff**
Video Training, Blog, Ebook, 3 Hour Presentation, Business Blueprints Etc.

**Low Price Offer**
Never Work Again, Outsourcing Mastery Books, 30 Min. Business Consulting

**Mid Range Offer**
DVD Boxset, Webinar Offers

**Continuity**
Work Less, Earn More Membership, Mr.Outsource University Membership

**Level 1 Backend**
Freedom Business Boot Camp - 3 Day Event

**Level 2 Backend**
Everything Above and Group Coaching

**Level 3 Backend**
Platinum Program, One-on-One Coaching, 7 Day Resort, Master Mind Group + Everything Above

Source: Information Marketing Funnel for Never Work Again (Bakke, 2013)
www.youwillneverworkagain.com

---

**See the Information Marketing Business Blueprint at**
www.youwillneverworkagain.com/bonus

---

The pros of this kind of work are that the products are potentially fast and easy to create, and entirely within your control. You get to offer something unique, and you can focus on an area you're passionate about and have expertise in  something which you are likely to consider part of your true path. It's also very profitable once you become good at it. However, the cons of information marketing are that it's very competitive because of the low barriers to entry, and it can take a long time to build up an audience and a reputation that are big enough to start making serious money. Once you're in that position, you really can feel as if you never need to work again; until you get there it can feel like a lot of hard work. In addition to this, because you are the brand, this is not really the kind of business that you can sell – while it's possible to build effective and efficient systems around information marketing of this type, it's almost impossible to automate it to the extent that you can fully remove yourself from the picture.

## From Thousands in Debt to Millions in Profit

To find out more about how information marketing works in practice, I got in touch with one of the undisputed kings of the industry, Mark Anastasi. Mark is the New York Times best-selling author of *The Laptop Millionaire*, a book that I strongly recommend for anyone looking to make money and give themselves a more positive mindset. When I talked to him he was in Slovakia, and getting ready to head to the Maldives for his honeymoon - "you have to go and see them before they sink into the ocean," he noted.

As is the case with a lot of entrepreneurs (myself included), Mark's story has humble beginnings, working as a security guard and in a dead-end sales job in Oxfordshire, UK, too afraid to return home to tell his parents in Cyprus that he was not the success they hoped he would be – in fact, he was £7,000 in debt and living in a squatted flat in London in 2004 when he attended his first personal development seminar and changed his life forever.

"It was that day that I realized I had a lot of very limiting beliefs about money, pretty common ones that my parents had passed on to me – like thinking that people with lots of money must be evil, or that you should spend what you have straight away so it doesn't get taken from you. So I started to get rid of those beliefs, and I wrote down all the ways I could think of to make money. I thought about a guy who was sitting next to me at the seminar earlier that day, who was bringing in a million dollars a year from online work. I had his number, so I rang him up and told him my situation – I said, I'm not asking for money, I will work for free for you, but I want you to teach me everything you know. And he told me, 'it's very simple – choose a target market and find out what solutions they need; offer them that solution in an ebook; create a website to sell it; and drive traffic to that website. If you can do all that, you'll make money'. So I got started over the next month."

And how long did it take for things to get going? "Well, my first ebook was about health topics – it took two weeks to research and write, a week to get the website done, and a few days integrating it with the ClickBank affiliate marketing website. The first day it sold no copies. The second day, one copy. The third day, two. And by the end of the week, it was up to five sales a day – all at $67 each. I launched another five books in the next year, and twenty-one the year after that, and by 2006 – two years after I was living in a squat – I was making over $450,000 in sales. I didn't even need to advertise anymore, because people on ClickBank were doing it for me in order to get their cut of the royalties. To date, I've sold about 40,000 ebooks worldwide."

From there, Mark went on to really master the concept of the information marketing funnel, building up his mailing list from the people that bought his books, and offering them more and more in-depth lessons and coaching. "You wouldn't ask someone to marry you on the first date," is how he puts it, "because they need to get to know you first and find out about all your great qualities. The same goes for your products – you can't expect customers to spend thousands of dollars at the start of your relationship. I was giving people information at a low cost in the beginning, but I found that more and more people were asking me for more, so I started putting on seminars in London and inviting the people on my list to come. Then people wanted DVDs of the seminars, so I started selling those. People wanted one-on-one coaching so I could help them with their specific situation, or they wanted to go on a retreat and watch me work for a few days, or have me watch them work and help them out. So all of these things came about, piece by piece – there wasn't a masterplan at the start, but it built up in stages."

As with many of the entrepreneurs I've talked to, outsourcing and leveraging other people's time is a big thing for Mark. Although he still writes his own mass emails - "I enjoy it, and it doesn't take much time," he says – he has a team of seven outsourced workers that focus on content creation, dissemination, and on driving traffic to his sites. "We have our own very automated process for creating content and sharing it across the web," he tells me, "called the Compound Growth 7 process, or CG7." I don't have the space to go into it here, but you can hear us discuss it in the full interview with Mark on my *Work Less, Earn More* membership site at http://www.youwillneverworkagain.com/experts/.

Ultimately, Mark says, the key to being a great information marketer is a desire to make a real difference in other people's lives through personal development. "We work hard – there are some fakers and 'get rich quick' schemes out there, but most of us emphasize hard work – to provide an alternative to being dependant on the government or listening to the corporate media. Money is really nothing but the measure of the value you provide to other people – if you create good content, money will come to you. And if you can get that content, that value, out to thousands of people, the money multiplies."

# Freedom Business Fact File

**Name:** Mark Anastasi
**Location:** London/Cyprus

**Where will you be in 5 years?:** I want to go from a seven figure business to an eight figure one, so I'm hiring a Director of Operations to help with that. Ultimately, I want to have the kind of place that Robert Kiyosaki currently has in popular culture – it's gonna be a lot of work!

**Software:** I use www.getresponse.com, a great autoresponder; GoToWebinar for my webinars; and subliminal power software, which flashes messages and affirmations on your screen so quickly that they only register in your unconscious mind – in 2005 I set it to say 'make $40,000 per month', and by early 2006 I was doing it.

**Gadgets:** I'm not really a gadget person, apart from my iPhone, but I do have a little thing called Pzizz, which is great – it helps you to relax and get to sleep much more quickly, and a 20 minute nap with this thing feels as refreshing as a two hour sleep.

**Where can we find out more?:** I have a blog and a mailing list at www.laptopmillionaire.tv, a free seminar DVD available at www.freemillionairemakerdvd.com, and if you check out www.freewebsitesinminutes.com we're giving away a tool to make – well, free websites in a few minutes, obviously. But join the list, there's always great stuff going on and you'll get to hear all about it.

For a different take on how information marketing could work I also reached out to a guy I've been working a lot with in recent months, Steven Essa. Steven is an absolute genius when it comes to using webinars for businesses, so I figured he'd have some important insights for us.

"It actually started when I was still employed for a real estate company," he told me, "and I was looking to get some speaking gigs to promote the company, and I went to a seminar about online marketing and ended up signing on to a $25,000 course. People thought I was crazy at the time, but six months later I'd generated over $100,000 for the company, and I decided to quit to build my own business. It's hard to get speaking gigs unless you have a lot of experience and a well-known name, so organizing speaking gigs myself in the form of webinars seemed like the way to go."

"I started off by practising with five or six friends and trying to sell them things, and then a week later did my first real webinar with around 15 people, and I made two sales at $297 each. A month later I was up to $4,000, then $10,000, and now one of my companies did a webinar a few weeks ago that made $120,000."

So for someone looking to use webinars in their info marketing business, how should they go about it? "It's fairly simple – you have useful information to give to people, so you put it together into a PowerPoint presentation and promote the webinar using a strong marketing hook, something like 'how to make $10,000 thanks to blogs'. Set it up on either GoToWebinar, which is $99 a month, or even just in Google Hangouts, and invite people from your list to attend. Then go through the content step-by-step, and make an offer at the end."

"We usually offer a book or a course at the end of the webinar to provide more information for the listeners. The conversion rate for a $30 book can be as high as 50% of the people in the webinar, but obviously you have to write the book in advance. If it's a course, there's maybe a 10% conversion rate, but you can wait until people sign up to start creating the content." And from there? "From that point on, your customers will usually make it clear what they want or need next from you."

Steven has a very interesting business model that he's been putting together for a few years now, and which makes the most of outsourcing principles. "When I started, I was working 14-16 hour days," he said, "and although I was making good money I didn't feel like that was right. So after a few years I started going into partnerships with other experts and helping them launch their businesses and owning half the business. So now I work with six companies, and I have various people working for me – one guy who does web design for all six, one on social media for them all, one doing the admin, and so on. I call it the 'medical centre model' – a medical centre rents out its space to doctors, and we rent out our expertise and resources to people so that they can concentrate on working with clients." In that way, Steven has helped others to create their own information marketing businesses, while avoiding one of the key pitfalls of the industry – too many people in this business end up with a brand that only revolves around them, and then suffer from working long hours and burnout.

"Webinars are so much better than just having a standard website, because they let you interact with potential clients, take questions, offer solutions, and build rapport and trust, which is key to closing sales. It can feel a bit awkward selling things to people at first, but as long as you have a product you believe in, by the end of your webinar you'll have the confidence to tell people what you're offering because they'll make it clear that they need and want help."

## Freedom Business Fact File

**Name:** Steven Essa
**Location:** Australia

**Where will you be in 5 years?:** I plan to be using the same model but with about 20 experts rather than the current 6, and with very streamlined procedures that let me spend two to four hours a month with each of them, like I currently do. Webinars are starting to grow exponentially as a niche, so I'd be crazy to walk away from it anytime soon.

**Software:** GoToWebinar, although it can be a little buggy at times; my own Webinator software that lets you record and play back webinars; PowerPoint or Keynote, the presentations I've made with those have brought in millions of dollars for me and my clients; Skype, of course; Screenflow, for recording webinars as well – it's just impossible to choose only three!

**Gadgets:** Apart from my iPhone, I'm very much a pen and paper kind of person, I don't use a lot of gadgets.

**Where can we find out more?:** You can check out my own webinar software that we've been developing for four years at www.webinator.biz, and I have a blog at www.stevenessa.com where you can sign up for our newsletter.

> **To hear the full interviews with Mark and Steven, go to**
> http://www.youwillneverworkagain.com/experts/

## Licensing

Licensing is perhaps the most complex of the ideas we're talking about here, but also the one with the biggest rewards if you get it right. In licensing, you are creating the big idea behind a product, and then licensing out the right to sell it to other entrepreneurs and businesses – you put in the hard work of developing the product, they put in the hard work of promoting and selling it, while you can relax and take a cut of royalties on each sale. An excellent example of how this can work in terms of licensing a business is my photography company. I started following my own advice and set up an efficient system that saw my company growing in popularity and reputation – the problem was that no matter how much you automate a system, photography still needs someone with talent to actually take the pictures. This meant I was stuck – I couldn't move around the world freely like I wanted to, because I needed to be where the photo shoots were taking place. So I basically licensed my business and the reputation it had built up to another professional photographer – he's taken over my existing contracts, and he and I bring new ones in on the back of our reputation. He does the majority of the work, but because I built the system in the first place, I get 30% of the income – and I have to do practically nothing for that money. Another option is to buy licenses yourself. Let's say you're on a trip to China and you see a cool product that you think could sell in the west – try to find out who makes it, get connected with them, and buy a license to sell it back home.

> ### See the Licensing Business Blueprint at
> www.youwillneverworkagain.com/bonus

The advantage of licensing is that much of the work of product development and R&D are outsourceable, while you can focus on networking and selling. The startup costs are also relatively low in comparison with the potential rewards. The cons are the potential legal complications – hence the need to have a relationship with a good lawyer – and the simple fact that it's quite difficult to come up with a good, innovative idea that will explode onto the marketplace. However, if you have a mind for creative thinking and an ability to follow through on your good idea, this could be the best of all the blueprints for you. I'd also recommend reading the book *One Simple Idea* by Stephen Key to give you more inspiration.

## Digital Products

In the case of digital products, you can either choose to create your own digital products or you can license them from others and resell them online. This can be music, ebooks, photography, apps, or anything else you can think of that people might want to buy over the internet. As with dropshipping, the initial difficulty will be in finding people that own products that are popular, but which they are willing to license to you rather than selling themselves or licensing to a more established business. Once you start to build up a reputation, this will become easier and easier, but as with all of these business models, you need to put in the work before you get to the point where you can make money while you sleep.

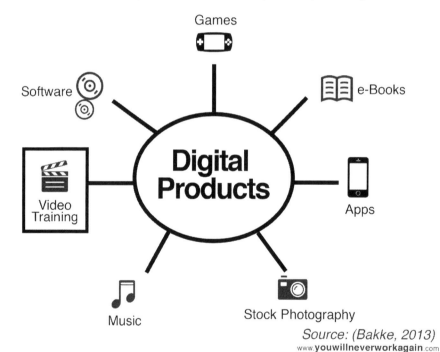

*Source: (Bakke, 2013)*
www.**youwillneverworkagain**.com

---

**See the Digital Products Business Blueprint at**
www.youwillneverworkagain.com/bonus

---

The pros of this model are that it's very laptop friendly, very scalable, and there's a huge number of distribution channels you can go through, thus easily increasing your visibility. A lot of the work is also outsourceable, and there's usually only a need for one licensing agreement that can be tweaked for different clients. The cons are that it's a very easy business model for other people to start work on as well, which means the competition is high – you're going to need to have some real marketing skills if you're going to become big in this line of work.

## Becoming a Best-Selling Author – Without A Publisher!

Looking for more information about how to get started with digital products, I got in touch with Simon Stanley and John Tighe, two guys with a lot of experience in this field. Simon started his online business career trying just about anything, from eBay selling to horse racing systems. "It was a nightmare," he told me, "But I knew that I wanted to avoid that corporate job route. So I was working minimum wage in a supermarket just to have enough money to come home and try to make more on the internet. Luckily, I had the drive to keep going, and not give in to tiredness like a lot of people who do that. Otherwise, I'd still be building wealth and value for other people rather than myself."

"My first experience selling digital products was when I got my little brother to write a guide for a video game that was big at the time. He was a bit of an expert at it, so I offered him £50 or a percentage of the profits. He took the £50, since I'd never really sold anything like this before. But people went crazy for it once I put it out there. Once you've made that first online dollar, you've broken a barrier in your mind – you've seen it's possible and you know you can make more."

After that, Simon started working on other ebooks on various topics – health, personal development, eBay selling. "Currently I have eight digital products on the go, and each of them has their own sales flow and marketing funnel – once you have existing customers, you should be offering something else to upsell to them, like videos. The most important thing is doing your research and finding out what's selling."

How can someone new to the digital products field do that? "Actually, doing some affiliate marketing first is a good idea – if you go to ClickBank and help someone else sell their product for a commission, you have proof that something is working. And when you find something that's selling, create your own version of it, and make it even better – most of the time that I've done that, the products have been surefire winners. A lot of good products out there have really poor sales videos or sales copy, so if you can improve on that, you can drive traffic to your site instead."

As I'm encouraging you to do, Simon outsources a lot of his tasks, and works on his own time. "I can usually tell pretty quickly whether I enjoy doing a task or not – whether it makes me feel like an employee or an entrepreneur. So customer service is outsourced so people can get a quicker response than if I was doing it myself; proofreading is outsourced; sometimes I outsource audio editing, and hopefully video editing in the future. Some people get their email lists managed by other people, but I enjoy that work. But I always do every task at least once myself, so that I know if other people are doing them the way I want. I get most of my freelancers through sites like Elance, and I tell them to come to me with any questions, and give them a link to their work afterwards so they can see how I'm using it – it helps to build a good relationship."

"I go through periods of maintenance and immersion with my work. Right now, I work about three or four hours a day, because

I'm trying to build the business. Other times, I might just focus on sending out emails, keeping traffic flowing to the sites, and networking, while I do other things with my life. But I always come back to the work in the end, because something inside me feels like I'm shrinking when I'm not creating value and living up to my full potential."

## Freedom Business Fact File

**Name:** Simon Stanley
**Location:** UK

**Where will you be in 5 years?:** Further ahead in terms of revenue, of course, but also in terms of influence and impact – I want to create a coaching program that will encourage people to live the freedom lifestyle.

**Software:** Camtasia for creating audio products; Final Cut Pro for editing video products; and Skype for keeping in touch with people, and for recording interviews with experts.

**Gadgets:** The only gadget I use is my iPhone – you can do everything on it, so what else do I need?

**Where can we find out more?:** Check out my blog, www.simonstanleysuccess.com, and for building an online business take a look at www.freedomincomeformula.com/free.

John Tighe is the author of the book *Crush It with Kindle* (and runs an online course with the same name), which gives people the inspiration and the skills to write and sell their own books online through Amazon. "I actually started as a corporate lawyer in the City of London, but I didn't really enjoy it, so I set up an online estate agency, which seemed like a good idea at the time. It didn't really work out, was very time intensive, and I had to pull the plug on it in January 2013 as I was actually losing money. But the experience did teach me a lot about marketing, which has now crossed over into the Kindle marketing side of things."

"I'd written a couple of books before," John told me, "but in the pre-internet days you really needed to get an agent and a publisher on board. But in 2012, I discovered Kindle Direct Publishing (KDP) and decided to try again, with a book about real estate. So now, getting published is the easy part – the Kindle website has a very simple two page wizard you go through, all you need is your manuscript and a cover image. The real work is in promoting it. That means a very clear, attention-grabbing title, nothing clever or cute that obscures the point – people don't have time for that. And you need a cover that pops off the page and will really stand out. Of course, none of this will work if you don't have a good book to promote that will deliver real value to your readers."

This, I already knew about. John has actually been helping me to promote this very book that you're reading right now. One of the key ways we did that was through split testing. We made a whole bunch of different covers, ran them as Facebook adverts, and tracked how many clicks each of them got. The current front cover turned out to be 338% more popular than the original one – that means the book has sold around an extra 11,000 copies just through having a better front cover.

But how much money can you really make from the royalties Amazon sends you from selling ebooks? "With *Crush It with Kindle* I sold 1100 copies in the first month, and made about $2000. But although the royalties are nice, the real money comes from other products and services – the books just set you up as an expert. From there, I have my online course, I do marketing for other people, and I have various other spin offs that wouldn't work without the book, but which make more money than the book – up in the five figure range per month."

"I don't have any permanent outsourced workers right now, but I find people on Upwork when I need book covers made, or on www.rev.com for audio transcriptions. But a lot of the infrastructure that would normally take up your time is provided by Amazon – they publish the books, and will even do some marketing for you once you start to sell enough copies. Then you can spend $30 a month for an autoresponder to email your list, and a bit more for a membership website – Kajabi is $99 a month for example, and very easy to use."

John left me with some final advice for would be writers: "Certain niches are never going to go away – health and well-being, personal finance, relationships and dating. So as long as you have good marketing,a  quality product, and you're targeting a decent sized market like these, you'll make sales. A lot of Kindle courses out there encourage you to churn out lots of crappy books, but I'm convinced that Amazon is going to start coming down hard on poor quality content like that someday fairly soon. It's bad for Amazon and it gives the whole self-publishing space a bad name. So don't do it – put in the time and effort to make something good, and you'll go much further. My other big tip would be – just get started! Sometimes things work, sometimes they don't, but you learn lessons from them either way, so don't put it off."

## Freedom Business Fact File

**Name:** John Tighe
**Location:** UK

**Where will you be in 5 years?:** I'm a big fan of Tony Robbins, and something he said that stuck with me is that it's difficult to project five years ahead in business as things change so fast today. I enjoy writing, teaching, consulting, and speaking – so I plan to still be doing those things.

**Where can we find out more?:** There are lots of free training videos about Kindle publishing at www.crushitwithkindle.com, and you can also find the book on Amazon, 'like' the Crush It with Kindle Facebook page, or subscribe to the YouTube channel.

> **The full interviews with Simon and John are available at**
> http://www.youwillneverworkagain.com/experts/

## Affiliate Marketing

In affiliate marketing, you are essentially promoting other people's products, and receiving a percentage of the sale price whenever a person buys that product because of you. So perhaps you have a blog on which you write about weightlifting, and an audience that respects and listens to your opinion on the topic (which could put you in a good information marketing niche). You recommend a particular protein shake, and give your readers a hyperlink they can click on to buy it – every time someone clicks on your link and buys the protein shake, you get a cut from the manufacturers. It's easy money, but, like information marketing, it only works after you've built up an audience that trusts you.

Source: (Commissionfactory)

**See the Affiliate Marketing Business Blueprint at**
www.youwillneverworkagain.com/bonus

The advantages of this work are that it is very easily done from a laptop, the work is outsourceable (particularly the research and writing of content), there's a lot of options for products and marketing channels, and there's no need for much in the way of legal agreements like patents or licenses. The disadvantages, as with many of these blueprints, is that the ease of the model makes it attractive to a lot of people, so competition can be high.

## ClickBank and Websites – Two Paths to Success

To get more information on how affiliate marketing could work for you, I reached out to two guys who make a lot of money from this work – Darren Stock, and Mike Omar. Darren is the author of *The ClickBank Affiliate Marketing Bible* - "ClickBank is a marketplace in which affiliates meet vendors," he explains, "so the vendor builds a product and the affiliate markets it and takes a commission for each sale. The commission varies, but on ClickBank it can often be up to 70%."

So once you have a product you like, how do you go about selling it? "Essentially, it's a case of driving traffic to a website, but it helps if you've done your research in advance and really know something about a particular niche before putting any money into it. When I started I was too eager and didn't bother doing enough of my own research – only to find out that the niche I was focusing on didn't really have much of a market. Once you have that research done, you need to know enough about search engine optimization (SEO) to make sure you can drive traffic to your sites without falling foul of the Google algorithm – I had a few sites disappear because of that in the beginning."

"After about six months of work, I had it cracked, and it's been plain sailing since then. At the moment, I have five sites that I'm driving traffic to – I used to have ten, but you don't want to spread yourself too thinly. Now I focus on making sure those sites get enough unique visitors a day to make the sales."

Unusually for most of the entrepreneurs I spoke to, Darren doesn't outsource any of his work, and has a cautionary tale about making sure you find the right people to work with. "I outsourced the SEO stuff in the beginning, but the people I got to do it were no good – they built poor quality links through forum commenting and that kind of thing, and eventually Google catches you out on that and your site disappears. Nowadays, because of the work I've put in, the whole business takes about four or five hours of my time each week, and I can spare that."

Darren did give me one more piece of advice before we finished talking – the power of using free ebooks as marketing tools. "I spend three hours a day on the train for my full-time job, and I know a lot about the subjects I'm writing on, so I use that time to put the books together. They're only about 7,000 to 10,000 words long because I don't like padding them out just for the sake of it – they're short and to the point, and I enjoy writing them, so they're an ideal tool really."

## Freedom Business Fact File

**Name:** Darren Stock
**Location:** UK

**Where will you be in 5 years?:** I have a few ideas in the pipeline, but I can't say too much right now – one is an app, and one will be a ClickBank product. But in general, I see this business as more of a hobby for me, and something I'll probably keep balancing with my full-time job.

**Software:** The ClickBank app on the iPhone; WordPress for building websites; DropBox, great for having regular access to my files; and an online tracking company called Bevo Media, which helps me keep track of which keywords are selling and which locations sales are coming from.

**Gadgets:** along with my iPhone, my Kindle – for pleasure, rather than business really, but it fits in the briefcase nicely and lets me read on the train.

**Where can we find out more?:** My website, www.darrenstock.com, and www.ebooksbydarren.com,

which will redirect you to my Amazon author page.

Like a lot of people, Mike Omar took his first steps into entrepreneurship after the company he worked for went under in the 2009 financial crash. "I started off doing all sorts of things," he told me on Skype from Barcelona, "working on websites for people, doing some catering, buying and reselling event tickets. With the event tickets thing, I realized there was no information online about how to do this kind of thing, so I wrote an ebook as a guide and set up a website to sell it. I'd almost forgotten about it, several months later, when the first sale came through – one book, and I made about $22 from it. Nothing really, but it showed me that making money online was possible."

From there, Mike took a different kind of path from the one Darren has focused on, with more of an emphasis on selling advertising space on high-ranking websites through Google AdSense. "In one year I built about 160 keyword-optimized websites, after doing some research to see which keywords were getting highly ranked. So, for example, if 'apartments in Barcelona' is a high ranking keyword on Google, then I make a website about apartments in Barcelona, put some relevant Google adverts on there, and every time someone clicks on of them, I get a cut of the advertising revenue. The problem is that your site needs to rank highly on Google to get enough traffic, so you have to use the Google Keyword Tool to find words that are popular but have relatively light competition. That takes time – I used to spend hours and hours a day doing it at first."

But once you have a site that's pulling in some good traffic, are there ways to further monetize things? "Definitely, you could add Amazon associate links for example – so if someone clicks through to a product on Amazon from your site, you make a cut of whatever they end up buying. Or you could use the sites for lead generation, building up a list that could be valuable to other companies in your niche."

"For the first year and a half, it was all just me – researching, building links, writing articles. But as soon as I could, I outsourced everything, which has given me the time to focus on my own teaching website and to travel. Things got outsourced pretty randomly at first, but now I have someone great, my VA Crystal in the Philippines. She is my point of contact for everything, and I trust her so much that I don't even bother to ask her what's going on, I just let her do it and I give her the money to pay the staff that she has working for her. And I work with an outsourced content company, and a couple of photographers in LA for an upcoming photography school project I'm working on."

Before we said our goodbyes, I had to ask Mike what was the deal with the name of his website, the Make Money From Home Lions Club? "I figured that lions are powerful and strong, but also quite lazy at the same time – a bit like me," he laughs. "It makes the site stand out from the crowd a little as well."

## Freedom Business Fact File

**Name:** Mike Omar
**Location:** All over the place

**Where will you be in 5 years?:** I guess one of my goals is to make $100,000 a month, just to see if I can really. That would have seemed ridiculous a few years ago, but not so much now – the only limits are the ones you set for yourself.

**Software:** WordPress for websites; Google Analytics for tracking traffic; Aweber for my mailing lists; Evernote is very useful.

**Gadgets:** My laptop, which has everything on it; and my guitar, which was a gift from an ex-roommate.

**Where can we find out more?:** You can learn more from my website www.makemoneyfromhomelionsclub.com. On the website you can learn exactly how to build a $5000 a month passive income website portfolio using my step-by-step video series and action plan, all 100% free via YouTube.

> **You can hear the full interviews with Darren and Mike at**
> http://www.youwillneverworkagain.com/experts/

## Multi-Level Marketing

There is one other idea for that came to my mind when writing this book, and this something that my good friend Øyvind Synnes does as a side-business. It's called multi-level marketing, and while it can take a while before you start making a permanent living from it, it can be a good way to learn the ropes as a new entrepreneur and to see how businesses are made up of a set of processes and systems. It's also a very good example of leveraging other people's time for your own benefit. You should be careful when entering a multi-level marketing scheme, as if you're too far down the hierarchy you can find that it's actually your time that is being leveraged – but if you get in reasonably early, it can be a good way of learning about business principles without a large investment.

Zinzino sells a range of coffee and health products, and Øyvind has been working with them since about 2009. "The company has a great culture and very good leadership, and we have a product that is sold on a subscription model, which helps us predict future income," he told me when we met up in Oslo.

"The set-up is very quick because you're buying into an existing model – the company provides the product and the contacts already. They provide training and a team leader to help guide you – essentially a free mentor – and you can invest anything between a few hundred dollars to about a thousand. And then you can sell the products directly to the consumer, or recruit other distributors – for each distributor you recruit, you take a commission."

So what do you look for in a new distributor? "It's the same qualities you need to look for in the leadership of a multi-level marketing company – hunger, passion, and good character. People you can see yourself building a relationship with, and people who have the tenacity to never give up, to never say no. And in terms of customers, anyone who likes coffee is a potential."

By recruiting other distributors to sell, while you take a commission, the whole business is essentially automated beyond the initial training. "There are people doing this full time for 15-30 hours a week, part timers doing 10-15 hours a week. Some people do maybe four hours a week, they get by with just a few meetings with their team. Things can get done quite quickly at the start, because you can sign up friends, family, and so on – after that, maybe it needs a bit more work to find customers."

"Ultimately, I love the freedom it gives me – but more importantly, I look forward to the relationships you build and the personal development the work offers."

## Freedom Business Fact File

**Name:**  Øyvind Synnes

**Location:** Norway

**Software:** I really like the online accounting program from Tripletex

**Gadgets:** Along with my Mac and iPhone, my new Tesla electric car – everyone should try one of them.

**Where can we find out more?:** Look me up on Facebook, LinkedIn, and Twitter.

---

**My full interview with Øyvind is available at**
http://www.youwillneverworkagain.com/experts/

---

Whichever business model you choose – whether one of the above, or something else – the important thing is that you fill out a blueprint for your idea, to help you systematize and organize it; and then you work out how to leverage other people's time as much as possible to run the business, leaving you free to concentrate on networking, marketing, growing the business, and, of course, following your own passions, while utilizing other people's time to get the more routine elements of the work done. There is one thing in common with all the business models, and that is the need to become an expert at sales and marketing. The success of your freedom business depends on it!

## Testing and Refining

Remember how I mentioned that current cover of this book converted 380% better than the older incarnations, and that helped to move an extra 11,000 units? That's an important example of one of the key things you should be doing in your business. Once you have a basic business system set up, from the absolute beginning you need to be testing and measuring it in order to be able to refine it and make it more efficient. Always 'cut the crap' – get rid of things that don't work or that you don't need. This applies to your business just as much as it should apply to your life. But the only way to know what's crap and what isn't is to measure and test things over and over again. I'm going to talk about this a lot more in the next few chapters, so for now let me just give you a basic example of the kind of thing I mean.

Whatever business model you've chosen, you're almost certainly going to have a website which you're using as a marketing and informational tool. You will be trying to make that website as visible as possible, probably through two methods – advertising through programs like Google AdWords, and using Search Engine Optimization (SEO) to make your website appear as high as possible up the search engine rankings for potential customers. However you're doing it, I feel fairly confident in saying that, in this day and age and with these kind of business models, you will be doing some digital marketing.

The basic principle here is that you should be experimenting with different ideas and – I cannot stress this enough – measuring the outcomes. Don't just pay for 10,000 views of a single advert on Google AdWords; get 2,000 views each of five differently worded adverts, and measure which one brings you the most sales. Focus on the advert that 'wins', but don't be afraid to try and refine it even further and do the same experiment again until you have the most effective online advert possible. I mentioned above that myself and John Tighe did this when deciding on a cover for this very book.

Another example is to use a technique known as 'A/B testing', which you can find in a book by Eric Ries called *The Lean Startup*. There's a number of companies online who offer to help you with this technique, although with a bit of ingenuity and website design knowledge, you might be able to put it together for yourself. The technique involves having two similar versions of the same website available to consumers – the products available are the same, but the design, layout, and copywriting are different on the two sites. The trick is to monitor which site does better in terms of converting visitors into sales, and then keep that design and discard the other.

Ultimately, the exact details of what you measure and how you measure it will vary for each business; but the important thing is to remember the principle – test things out, measure their effectiveness, refine your systems accordingly. This is a key skill for any entrepreneur to understand and utilize.

## In The Next Section

Now that we've discussed some of the basics of getting started in business, the next three chapters will discuss the nuts and bolts of business in more detail. Specifically, I want to show you how to run a business that makes you money without monopolizing your time. In chapter five, we'll look at some basic principles that will help you run a more efficient business, and then in chapters six and seven we'll look at the two major techniques that I apply to my business – automation and outsourcing. These chapters are in part written for people who are already at the third level of entrepreneurship – they have businesses up and running, but feel trapped by how much of their time is taken up by those businesses. These chapters will help you start to put in place some principles that will, over time, reduce the hours you need to work to keep your business running smoothly. However, if you've just read this chapter and have some great ideas for potential businesses, but you haven't got started yet, please feel free to read on – the sooner you put these principles and techniques into action when you build your business, the better; so if you learn about them now, when you're just getting started, you'll already be ahead of the competition.

Want to learn even more about business blueprints and starting your freedom lifestyle? Then Check out my free training videos at http://www.worklessearnmore.tv/.

## Resources

Mark Anastasi, *The Laptop Millionaire: How Anyone can Escape the 9-5 and Make Money Online* (John Willey & Sons, 2012) - Lots and lots of great ideas on how to make money online.

Michael E. Gerber, *The E-Myth Revisited: Why Most Businesses Don't Work and What You Can Do About It*, (HarperCollins, 2013) - A must read for all entrepreneurs on how to make your business work without you.

Dan S. Kennedy, *How to make Millions with your Ideas* (Plume, 1996) - A brilliant book with tons of business ideas. If you have not found a solution above then this is the book for you.

Stephen Key, *One Simple Idea: Turn Your Dreams Into a Licensing Goldmine While Letting Others Do the Work* – a great primer on how to leverage other people's time while building a business based on licensing.

Brett McFall, *How to Make Money While You Sleep: A 7 Step Plan for Starting Your Own Profitable Online Business* (Wrightbooks, 2008) – A great book about information marketing.

Chad Mureta, *App Empire: Make Money, Have a Life, and Let Technology Work For You* – an excellent run-through of how to make a decent income through mobile phone apps – if you're thinking of taking on the licensing blueprint, this is a must-read.

David Kord Murray, *Borrowing Brilliance: The Six Steps To Business Innovation by Building on the Ideas of Others* – an interesting and important examination of how innovation happens by building on the works of those who have gone before us.

Alexander Osterwalder & Yves Pigneur, *Business Model Generation: A Handbook for Visionaries, Game Changers and Challengers* (John Wiley & Sons, 2010) - This book is the basis for the framework we used in this chapter and it's used all over the world to train entrepreneurs in systems and business thinking.

Eric Ries, *The Lean Startup: How Constant Innovation Creates Radically Successful Businesses* – a very detailed and informative introduction to the processes of refining your system and innovating to increase your profits.

Alexander Sinclair, *The Dropshipping Guide: How to Start Your Dropshipping Business Without the Learning Curve* (Amazon, 2012) - A more in depth guide on how to make money from dropshipping.

Robert Skrob, *The Official Get Rich Guide to Information Marketing: Build a Million Dollar Business in 12 Months* (Entrepreneur Press, 2011) – A step-by-step guide on how to start an information marketing business from scratch.

Antoine Walker, *How I Make $10 million from Internet Affiliate Marketing*, (CreateSpace, 2012) – An easy to read book about affiliate marketing.

# Links

The sample business blueprint canvas comes from *Business Model Generation* by Alexander Osterwalder and Yves Pigneur – it's available on a Creative Commons licence, so feel free to download it at http://www.businessmodelgeneration.com/downloads/business_model_canvas_poster.pdf [http://tinyurl.com/bizmodcanvas] and use it for your own projects. The same goes for the business blueprints that I created from their canvas!

Finally, to hear the full versions of the interviews quoted in this chapter, head over to http://youwillneverworkagain.com/experts/ – they're all on there, and range from around twenty minutes to over an hour, so there's sure to be some nuggets of wisdom to help you which I simply didn't have space for here.

# CHAPTER 5

# Time: Your Most Precious Resource

*"Time is free, but it's priceless. You can't own it, but you can use it. You can't keep it, but you can spend it. Once you've lost it you can never get it back."*

~Harvey MacKay

If you followed the advice in the last chapter, you should now have a blueprint for your own business – either using one of the pre-made templates I linked to, or by filling in a blank template with your own business ideas. For many people, this is where the problems start. They have no problem coming up with ideas for businesses, or even getting them off the ground – but once they're running, they take up every waking hour of their time, and leave them stressed out, endlessly busy, and unable to live life on the level they want. Maybe they end up making a good amount of money, but what's the point if there's no time to enjoy it?

That's where this chapter, and the next two, come in. I'm going to show you how to take your existing business and automate, outsource, and systematize it to become more profitable while taking up less of your time. It sounds too good to be true, but it's perfectly possible. I've done it myself, but while it took me years of trial and error, you'll be getting exactly the same knowledge just by reading a few chapters in a book. The next two chapters deal with the two main techniques I've used to achieve this in my own life – automation and outsourcing – but this short chapter focuses instead on four major principles that I think you need to keep in mind at all times if you're aiming to never work again.

## Letting Things Fail

This principle sounds a little counter-intuitive – if you want to succeed, then surely the last thing you want is to fail? But try thinking of it another way. I spent years trying and failing to work out the perfect systems for my businesses, and it was only from failing so much that I learned how to succeed. Getting things wrong is the best way to learn, as long as you're willing to analyze your mistakes and ensure that you don't repeat them. Ninety percent of all businesses set up by entrepreneurs fail within the first five years. It doesn't seem that way sometimes, but that's because we only hear about the success stories. The bad news is that this means there is a good chance that your business will fail – maybe because you didn't get it quite right, maybe because of something that's out of your hands (although hopefully reading this book will help decrease your chances of failure). The good news is that you're not going to be the only one, so there's no need to take it too personally. Pick yourself up and try again, either with a new idea in which you incorporate the lessons you learned, or with a refined and improved version of your original plan.

The most important thing is not to become downhearted or despondent because of your failures. Instead of seeing them as the end of the road, or as a door closing on you, think of them as an opening, or a new beginning – a chance to learn, to improve and to do things differently next time. As Malcolm Forbes, the publisher of the famous magazine, said, "failure is success if we learn from it".

Let me give you a story from my own business to illustrate this point. In the last chapter I told you how I started to licence my photography business to a another guy. Well, shortly after this, we landed a big contract with the Norwegian company Helly Hansen – and when I say big, I'm talking around £100,000 a year. I'd been training my new partner for some time using my company's own information marketing product, *The Secrets of 360 Photography*, and by working with him on some of our other clients. But at this time I was in San Francisco, far from the action, and I thought it was time that I let him walk for himself  and take on this big contract for himself. I won't go into the details, but needless to say mistakes were made, and we ended up losing the contract. I could have got mad, I could have thrown things across the room, I could have immediately withdrawn our licencing agreement; but none of those things were going to bring that massive contract back. So instead, I called a meeting with him, and we discussed what had gone wrong and how to learn from the experience. Essentially, I had to tell myself that although I'd lost £100,000, my partner and I had gained an invaluable amount of education and knowledge about how to improve. And we must have learned well, because things have improved immeasurably since that day.

Thomas J. Watson once said "Recently, I was asked if I was going to fire and employee who made a mistake that cost the company $600,000. No, I replied, I just spent $600,000 training him. Why would I want somebody to hire his experience?" He had the right idea. Helping other people deal with failure and helping them to understand their mistakes and improve on them adds value to the world. The people you help are going to better workers in the future because of it, and they're going to be loyal to you and enthusiastic for the work that you do because you helped them to make that improvement. Shouting, screaming, and tearing people down, on the other hand, is just destructive. And if this goes for other people, it also goes for yourself – don't beat yourself up for your failures, but think clearly about where you went wrong. You'll be much better for it in the future.

Managing failure well is one of the most important skills an entrepreneur can have, because you can only have as much success as you're willing to fail for. Succeeding means taking chances, and taking chances means putting yourself at risk of failure. But if you want to experience massive success, you have to take the biggest chances, and be prepared for the possibility for equally massive failure. And then you have to be ready to pick yourself up and start again.

## The Pareto Principle

This all links with another important idea – the Pareto Principle. This principle is named after Vilfredo Pareto, an Italian economist from the early 20th century, who noted that in most of the cases he observed, 80% of all the results came from only 20% of the effort – 80% of the peas in his garden came from 20% of the pods, for example. In business, this is usually taken to mean that 80% of your sales will come from 20% of your clients, but we could also say that 20% of the effort you are putting into your business on a normal day is producing 80% of the positive results. The thing you should be trying to identify when setting up and refining your system is what that 20% consists of – then you should focus your efforts exclusively on that, and automate or outsource the other 80% of your effort to the greatest extent possible.

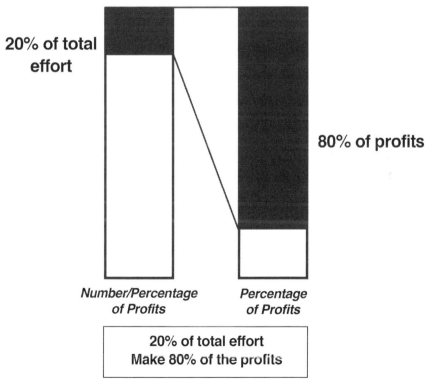

*Source: 80/20 Principle (Bakke, 2013)*

It probably sounds scary at first, the idea of giving away 80% of your work to other people, who could get it wrong. But here's the thing – firstly, much of that work is going to be simple but time-consuming stuff, which any relatively well-educated and well-balanced person can manage to complete successfully. And secondly, if you've done this right, almost all of the work that you're giving away is relatively unimportant – it is the part of the work which is necessary, but which produces only 20% of the final results. Even if the people you delegate to get some of the work wrong, the long-term effect is minimal and easily fixable by hiring more competent employees. In the meantime, you're working on the really important 20% that will grow your business further.

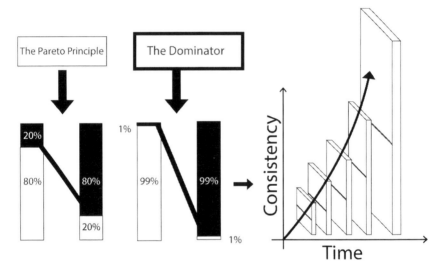

The Dominator principle is where you need to focus as a fresh entrepreneur.
Figure out 1 thing that works, then consistently repeat it over time for dominance.

*Amazon.com ONLY sold books for the first 5 years they were in business. Then they made the "crazy" decision to start selling DVD's!

Source: (Bakke, 2013)
www.youwillneverworkagain.com

The Pareto Principle dovetails nicely with what I call the 'dominator principle' – the idea that you should find the one thing you do extremely well, and then focus on it until you dominate the competition. For example, Amazon only sold books for the first five years of their existence. They were good at selling books, they knew what they were doing, and they eventually became so dominant in the online book market that they could start to branch out into other products with much less risk to their bottom line. Of course, I don't need to tell you how well that went for them. This is like the Pareto Principle in it's most extreme form – focus on the most important 1% of your business. The advantage of this approach is that your consistency compounds. This is shown on the right hand side of the diagram above – by focusing on the one thing you are great at, you will become better and better at an exponential rate. Consistency, combined with time, will be the key to your success.

I'll try to make this even clearer with a final example. Think of a sailboat – a huge, heavy object, and if you could stand on the water and push it from the side, you wouldn't be able to budge it by an inch, no matter how strong you are. And yet, you can move the rudder from side to side with one finger, and – voila! - the boat moves immediately and with ease. This is the whole idea behind the Pareto principle – the smallest amount of effort can have the biggest difference, if it's applied in the right places. You just need to find what those places are, and concentrate your efforts on them.

## Own a System, Not a Job

I talked a lot about the importance of building systems in the last chapter, but it really can't be emphasized enough – building effective systems for leveraging other people's time is the way to never work again. Building a system means you have something that will continue to work effortlessly even when you're not paying full attention to it. I'd even say that building an effective system is your duty as an entrepreneur – if you don't have a replicable system that can work on other people's time, then you're not a real entrepreneur; if your business dies when you die, the value your business creates in the world dies with you. I want to introduce a couple of ideas here to really drive this point home.

# CASH CRUNCH PYRAMID

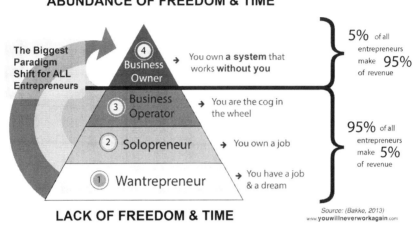

**ABUNDANCE OF FREEDOM & TIME**

The Biggest Paradigm Shift for ALL Entrepreneurs

4 Business Owner → You own **a system** that works **without you**

3 Business Operator → You are the cog in the wheel

2 Solopreneur → You own a job

1 Wantrepreneur → You have a job & a dream

5% of all entrepreneurs make **95%** of revenue

95% of all entrepreneurs make **5%** of revenue

**LACK OF FREEDOM & TIME**

Source: (Bakke, 2013)
www.youwillneverworkagain.com

This is the Cash Crunch Pyramid, and it shows you the different kinds of entrepreneur that I discussed all the way back in the introduction. At the bottom we have wantrepreneurs, the people who have a lot of ideas but haven't got started yet. The last chapter should have given you some motivation to get out of this level. The next level up is the solopreneurs – those who are essentially self-employed. They work for themselves, but they have no employees and they don't leverage other people's time at all. If they stop working, the business stops generating money. The third level is the operators. They run bigger businesses, and are in charge of employees who take on some of the workload. In theory, they can go on holiday for a week or two without the business collapsing. But that's all – if they stop concentrating on the boring day-to-day tasks of the business for too long, things will fall apart. The businesses that operators run are too caught up with their own personal qualities – they are not systems that can operate without the input of the person at the top.

I estimate that the three lower levels of the pyramid make up around 95% of all entrepreneurs. At the same time, they bring in only 5% of all the revenue that entrepreneurs make. None of them are really making much more than the average person with a job, but they all have a lack of time and a lack of freedom. They might even be less free than the guy with a boring old desk job – at least he can go home and forget about work until the next day, whereas these three levels of entrepreneurs often feel like they're on call 24/7. This is why it is imperative that you make the shift to the top of the pyramid – becoming a business owner.

Business owners may superficially appear to be the same as business operators. But while the operator is inextricably linked with the daily work of his company, the owner is removed from it. The business owner is in charge of a system, rather than being a part of it. All the individual roles in the system are taken by others. From the little things like answering phone calls and emails, to the big things like fulfilling orders and creating marketing materials – all of them are taken care of by people who know how to perform their role, and are happy to do so in exchange for a regular wage. The business owner, meanwhile, brings in high levels of profit, is able to scale the business up easily by hiring more people, and can construct a life based around the activities they love. And because the day-to-day activities of the business are taken care of by others, all they have to do is keep an eye on things to ensure they are running smoothly. People at this level of the Cash Crunch Pyramid make up only about 5% of all entrepreneurs, but are bringing in 95% of all entrepreneurial revenue because of the ability to scale their business systems and take advantage of new opportunities. Perhaps most importantly, they also have a lot of time and a lot of freedom to live the life they want. This is where you want to be, and this is where I aim to help you reach.

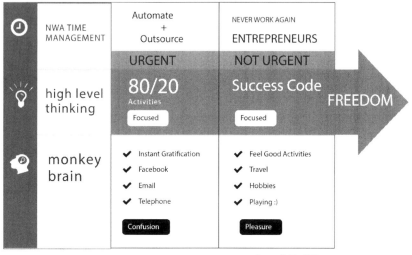

Source: (Bakke, 2013)
www.youwillneverworkagain.com

The second diagram I want to introduce you to is above. It looks a little complicated at first, but I'll walk you through it – it's essentially a diagram about time management. Essentially, we can split all of our activities across two spectra. Firstly, things can be seen as either urgent or not urgent. By urgent, I'm not necessarily talking about importance – something that is urgent is something that grabs your attention and insists you attend to it right away, no matter what its level of importance. And things that are non-urgent are those that we feel we can delay or push to the side for now – even if they're important, they don't clamor loudly for our attention in the same way that the urgent things do, so we can end up neglecting them if we don't manage our time to include them. Secondly, we can divide our tasks into those that use higher level thinking, and those that engage our 'monkey brain'. Thanks to evolution, humans have the capacity to think some very complicated thoughts, which is how we've achieved so much over the course of our civilizations; but we're still not so different from our monkey ancestors. There's still a less evolved part of our brain that wants to focus less on abstract, conceptual thinking and more on the simple pursuit of pleasure and attending to the stimuli that are immediately in front of us. Let's see how this maps out, and what you should do about it.

Towards the bottom left of the diagram we see the things that are urgent and which engage our monkey brain. These are the immediate stimuli that are put before us every day, which send the less evolved bit of our brain into confusion as we desperately try to keep up. I'm talking about phone calls, the 'ping' of another email landing in our inbox, the distraction of ending up on Facebook checking out our friends' pictures, and so on. You need to be reducing the amount of time you spend on these – I'm not saying you should never slack off a little, but the daily grind of phone calls and emails should be for employees, not for the business owners.

Above that we have activities that are also urgent, but which are based more around high level thinking. This includes meetings, dealing with crises and problems, and directing your staff on a daily basis. You're probably thinking that this is the kind of stuff an entrepreneur should be dealing with regularly, but I would suggest that this is the wrong way to look at it. With activities like this, you should be implementing the Pareto Principle that we discussed above. Determine the 20% of your business that is making the most profit and focus on, putting the other 80% to the side. Then focus on the most important 20% of that work, and leave the remaining 80% to your staff. I don't sit in on every meeting that happens in my businesses, I don't spend all day telling my staff what they should do, and I try to minimize the amount of time I spend dealing with anything that could be called a 'problem'. In this way, I leverage other people's time to deal with the left-hand column of 'urgent' things, giving me more time to focus on the other side of the equation – the non-urgent things that can be forgotten otherwise.

Let's have a look at that now. On the bottom right, we have monkey brain activities that are less urgent. This includes our hobbies, our travel, the time we spend playing, looking after ourselves, and hanging out with friends and family. These things can often have less of an obvious, immediate pull than the distracting monkey brain activities of email, smart phones, and the internet, but they're much more necessary in our life. By the time we're finished here, you should have much more free time to enjoy these activities which will nourish you in mind, body, and soul. Above that we have the high level activities that are not urgent. These include relationship building and networking, researching and taking advantage of new business opportunities, product development and brainstorming, and employee training. We all know that these things are important as well as being some of the most enjoyable work activities – but when faced with an onslaught of urgent tasks, it can be easy to place them to one side and get ourselves caught up in a spiral of never-ending distraction. We never get the time to pick up those important tasks again, our business never grows beyond its current state, and we never free ourselves from our work. The rest of this book is devoted to getting you on the path to freedom – reducing the amount of time you spend on daily, urgent tasks, giving you more time to spend on both the pleasures of life and on these important activities that will help your business grow.

## Less is More

If your system is going to be efficient, you need to take this principle into account. You might pimp your ride, but don't pimp your business. Many people associate the world of business with luxury – fancy buildings, expensive furniture, first class flights every week, that kind of thing. And it's true that in the past, and even today to some extent, the people at the very top of the business ladder live that way. But you're not at the top of the ladder yet, and if you spend loads of money on unnecessary expenses in order to pretend that you're at the top, you never will be. Your system really should be operating on the most minimal basis that it possibly can, because that is the way that you are going to make maximum profit for minimum effort. Every $500 office chair you buy to give off an impression of luxury represents extra hours of work that you're going to have to put in to further increase your revenue to make up for your silly purchases. Don't do it, it's not worth it – value your time above your pride. My businesses operate minimally – I make sure my staff are comfortable and have everything they need to do their jobs to the best of their ability, but I don't bother to rent gleaming office buildings in the downtown areas of famous cities, because I know that I don't need that. My businesses work perfectly well operating from smaller, cheaper offices, so why increase my expenses by 300% by upgrading?

These four principles are some of the cornerstones of my businesses – they are four of the most important things that I try to keep in my head the whole time when I'm building a new business. In the next chapter we'll look at one of the major techniques I've used in order to free myself from work and make my business more efficient – building an automated system. Keep the principles we've discussed in this chapter in your mind, and you'll see that they clearly apply to everything I'm going to talk about next.

> *"Genius is one per cent inspiration, and
> ninety nine per cent perspiration"*
>
> ~Thomas Edison

You can find more of my tips and tricks for using your time more efficiently in my training videos at http://www.worklessearnmore.tv/.

## Resources

Stephen R Covey, *The Seven Habits of Highly Effective People: Powerful Lessons in Personal Change* (Free Press, 1989)

Robert Kiyosaki, *Rich Dad, Poor Dad* (Plata Publishing, 2011) – Kiyosaki expertly lays out the difference in mindset between the people who work for money, and the people who have money work for them. A must-read for people who want to own a system, rather than a job.

Rich Koch, *The 80/20 Principle: The Secret of Achieving More With Less* (Nicholas Brealey Publishing, 1997)

**CHAPTER 6**

# Business Autopilot

*"We are what we repeatedly do.*
*Excellence, then, is not an act,*
*but a habit"*

~ Aristotle, Nicomachean Ethics
(paraphrased in Will Durant's The Story of Philosophy)

## What is Automation?

Throughout this book so far, the one thing I have tried to make clear more than anything else is the need for you to develop efficient systems that your business revolves around. A business is essentially a set of processes and actions which aim to create value for the customer and the business owner. The difference between a business operator who is trapped by his work, and the business owner who is liberated from it, is the ability to turn those processes into systems – that is, to make them standardized and repeatable. A system is something predictable, something in which the processes and actions are performed in the same way every single time. The great advantage of a system like this is that other people can be trained to perform most of the processes and actions that make up the system. This means you are free to do whatever you want, safe in the knowledge that your business continues to function even without your watchful eye constantly trained on it.

Furthermore, by having a system in place, you are following the Pareto principle – 20% of your work is producing 80% of your results, so it makes perfect sense to set your business up so that the other 80% of the work happens easily and efficiently and takes up as little of your time as possible. With an efficient system in place for your basic business processes, you can focus on the 20% of your business that most requires your input – networking, creative thinking, marketing, and finding new opportunities to expand and grow, as well as having time to devote to your own personal development.

Building a system that works on other people's time without the need for your continued input is what I mean when I say 'automation'. In this chapter I'm going to provide a number of suggestions for how to do this – these can be applied to an existing business if you have one, or, if you're starting a new business, they can easily integrated into your planning to make sure that business works as well as it can from the very start. It is hard work, and it will require a lot of time and careful thinking and planning at the beginning, but this is relatively short term. Compared to having a chaotic and inefficient business that requires your constant attention, the work you put in to automate your business will be short term and will definitely pay off over time. Think of it as delayed gratification, which is a good thing to apply throughout your life as well as your business – if you can stay disciplined at the start, the rewards will be greater.

# *Exercise:*
## *The World's Most Simple System Builder*

*First of all, most entrepreneurs go 'oh shit, I have to make a system now? I don't have time for that!'. That's right, and that's why you find somebody to build your system for you. Be creative – there is somebody out there that can create your system for you. I have my systems made by my employees, I don't build them myself. However I have built lots of systems before, and here is the most simple way to do it. Imagine you are a chef and need to make your customers a dish (deliver a service or a product). What do you do?*

**What you need to make product/service**
**+**
How to put it together
_____
**Result that you measure**

*Source: Recipe Creation Methodology (Bakke, 2013)*
www.**youwillneverworkagain**.com

- *You start by figuring out what kind of ingredients you need to make the dish. Choose a process in your business where there is no system in place and write down a list of ingredients you need to deliver your service/product.*

- *Once you have your list you need to explain step-by-step how you will be putting it together in the right order and combinations.*

- *Test and measure the result so you know it's up to your standard.*

## Cook Book Systems Creation Method

> Title + Simple Description

**Picture of Finished Product**     **Ingredients:**              **How to put it together:**
                                    - widget                      1) write down the first step
                                    - widget  x 2                 2) write down the second step
                                    - widget x 4 etc.             3) etc.
                                    - etc                         4) etc.
                                    - etc                         5)
                                    - etc
                                    -etc

**How to serve the product/service to the client;**
1)
2)
3)

**What and how to measure (quality of delivery)**
1)
2)
3)

**How to Video**
\* A simple screen recording or iphone is enough .
You are not aiming for an academy award...

*Voila! You have just created your first system for you business. I've provided a helpful little recipe sheet above for you to do this for your own business. Just pick the most time consuming part of your business, or the bit you least want to keep doing, and work out how to build a system for it. Once you have created enough recipes, you have a company operating manual, and this document becomes the backbone of everything you do in your business. It makes every single person in your business replaceable, because based on the manual anybody can do the work of everybody in your company. It will also save you a lot of times in regards to training – without this kind of document, you will have to spend the time training new members of staff. It's tedious work to create it – but think about all the time you will be saving in the future. The better the recipe book for your business, the more freedom you will have.*

**I also talk about this exercise in one of my tutorial videos at**
http://youwillneverworkagain.com/exercises/

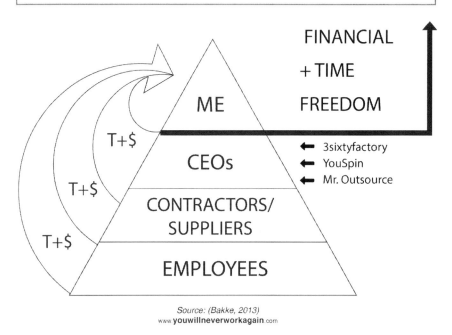

*Source: (Bakke, 2013)*
www.**youwillneverworkagain**.com

Take a look at the diagram above, which shows the benefits of automating your business and leveraging other people's time. In this pyramid, you're at the top – below you are your employees, your suppliers and contractors, and the CEOs of your business. Each of them is contributing a certain amount of their own time to your business in a way which will benefit you monetarily. Your employees are putting in the most time, and probably making you the most money due to their fixed wages, whereas your income is based on the performance of the business. Your products, whether physical goods or digital or information products, are being made by suppliers, contractors and freelancers – their time is used rather than yours, but you make a profit when the products get sold. And then your CEOs, who are making more money than the rest of the pyramid due to their skills, but still putting in their time and effort to ensure everything tuns smoothly. And as you can see on the left hand side of the pyramid, all of that time and money works its way upwards to the business owner. Ultimately, freedom comes down to time and money – other people's time becomes your money.

## Habits

The most important element of long term success is habits. Habits are the little actions that are repeated regularly, and which seem to have only a very small effect individually, but which add up to something much more important over time. We naturally tend to think of our lives in terms of 'big moments'. But most of our life is made up of small actions and small decisions, which contribute to a greater whole. Here's an example – if you've ever taken the London Underground, you know that it has a lot of escalators to get between the ground level and the platforms, and that most people will stand still on these escalators on the right hand side. I, however, walk up or down the moving escalator on the left hand side. On any individual occasion, this is not something that I find difficult or exhausting – it's just a few steps after all. But if I walk 100 stairs per day because of this minor habit, annually that comes to 36,500 more steps than people just standing on the side on the way to the gym, and that's going to give me a healthier heart and a happier old age. All because of this one little habit that seems so insignificant each time I do it. Little things add up.

Another example is that of compound interest, which has been called "the eighth wonder of the world". If you put $10,000 in a savings account, you earn more and more each year on that money even if the interest rate remains the same. Your habits are the same

– they compound. Small choices made today, and every day that follows, will eventually add up to have large impacts on your life. For example, most people complain about not having time to read books. However if you read 10 pages per day (5-10 minutes) that's 3,650 pages per year. That's about 12 books a year!

Just like you should be conscious of your larger choices in life – like considering what makes you happy and unhappy, or what your true path is – you should also try to be conscious of your small choices in life, your habits, and direct them towards things that will contribute to your happiness. That doesn't mean acting 'perfectly' at all times, it just means being conscious about what you are choosing to do – you may choose to continue standing on the right hand side of the escalator, because you prefer the convenience of the moving staircase to the slight health benefits of walking up the steps. That's fine, but do it because you've consciously decided to do it, rather than simply sleepwalking through life.

It's estimated to take around ninety days, or thirteen weeks, to ingrain a new habit. That means that habits that seem difficult at first become almost second nature if you use your willpower to stick with them for ninety days. If the changes you're making to your habits are going to make you live a happier, healthier life, those ninety days of willpower and difficulty are undoubtedly worth the effort. It's delayed gratification again – you may not feel any benefit from the changes immediately, but you will in time. That's why 'The Reverse Gap' exercise we did in chapter two is so important, to help you realize and celebrate the steps you've taken and the improvements you've made.

# The Success Code

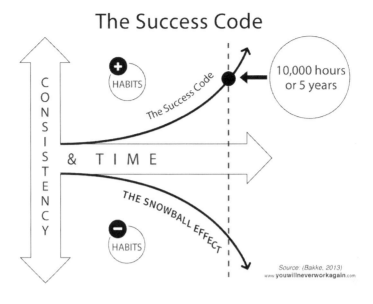

Source: (Bakke, 2013)
www.youwillneverworkagain.com

The diagram above shows what I mean. Creating habits takes consistency over time – you need to keep doing the same thing, and you need to keep doing it regularly. As long as your habits are positive, helpful ones, every time you do them you are working towards success. Eventually, those positive habits will just be another part of your life – something you do as naturally as breathing. I've pointed to the 10,000 hour mark on the diagram, which Malcolm Gladwell has famously said is the point at which you become an 'outlier', someone who is exceptionally good at a particular activity. Each time you act on your habits, you're moving towards that point, and even if you never reach it, you're at least going in the right direction. At the same time, be aware of bad habits – if you consistently repeat bad habits like sleeping in, eating unhealthily, watching TV and so on, they will also compound and send you on a downwards spiral – or a 'snowball effect' as I've called it. A lot of this is fairly common knowledge, but the problem is that it isn't common practice – we know we should have good habits and we know we should get rid of our bad ones, but very few of us do anything about that. If more people did, they would find themselves being a lot more successful.

One more concrete example of how habits are formed and how they bring success – I talked earlier about my meditation practice, and all the benefits it has brought to me – but that's a habit like any others, and it needed to be consciously built. Like most people, I didn't meditate daily, so when I decided that meditation might be able to help me, I needed to start from scratch. That meant I had to stop thinking about doing it, and start actually doing it; and it meant continuing to do it daily even when it seemed like a chore or an irritation. At times, the need to meditate every day seemed like a distraction from my work; at times it seemed like it was bringing me no benefits, and I could just throw it away with no negative consequences. But through willpower, and reminding myself everyday of the benefits I hoped to gain through this habit, I managed to keep doing it until, one day, without even realizing it consciously, it was just another part of my routine, as natural as brushing my teeth; and it was a part of my daily routine that brought me great benefits, as I've already discussed.

Here are some tips on ways to make changing your habits easier:

- Peer groups. You are defined by the people you surround yourself with, the people you interact with regularly. So make sure that your peer group has similar interests to you. If you want to change a particular habit, you could convince a friend to change at the same time, and encourage each other; or you could find a new group of people who are interested in that habit, and spend time with them. For example, if you want to go running every day to improve your health, take a friend with you and share the benefits – or find a running group in your city and hang out with like-minded people who will encourage you to reach your goals.

- Journals. Write down your progress every day on each habit you're trying to change. If you're trying to run every day, write down how far you went, what your route was, and, perhaps most importantly, how you felt. This is a good idea not just for organizing your thoughts, but also for referring back to at a later date. Don't feel like running today? Have a look at your journal for yesterday and remember how good it made you feel – suddenly you'll find yourself a lot more motivated to go again.

- Making things visible. If you make things visible, you're more likely to do them. So keep a visual cue somewhere near you to remind you about your new habits. For a runner, this could be something as simple as keeping your sweatbands in a visible location, or putting your running shoes in the middle of the floor so that every time you step over them on the way to do something else, you remember 'that's right, I still need to go running today'.

These three techniques can apply to anything, not just running – whatever your new habits are, you'll find encouragement by hanging out with the right people, writing your thoughts down, and making things visible.

Here are my daily habits that have proved to work very well for me; although I'm always optimizing my habits, so they may have changed when I meet you! The most successful people throughout history, such as Benjamin Franklin, have always understood that setting up good habits and being consistent with them over time is the key to success. You should now be inspired to do the same! Yes, it does take time for me to go through these habits, and I could spend that time on work instead to get short-term benefits like more customers – but I view these habits as a long-term investment in myself, as a cost of being an entrepreneur. It's almost like a business expense, to keep myself healthy and grounded. The time I spend on it is justified, at least to my mind, because I'm in it for the long run.

| Daily Rituals | Mind | Body | Food |
|---|---|---|---|
| Morning | - 30 Min Pranayama Meditation<br>- Daily Magic Walk 15 Min.<br>*Based on Tony Robbins method called daily magic. Bonus track on get Get The Edge. 1. incantations 2. gratitude 3. future attraction 4. incantations. If you only have 5 minutes in the morning then do 5, the 10 later etc. Just fit it in... | - P90X iPad (1hour) 3 - 5 times a week<br>* Makes it possible to exercise all<br>over the world no matter where you are. Great system!<br>- Jogging and Cycling<br>* I may exchange a P90X day for other activities. | -0.5 Liters of water when I wake up<br>* Rehydrates, cleanses and gets your bowls working to get rid of waste<br>- Juicing/Green Smoothie 10 Min.<br>* Alternate every other day to give body fibre as well as pure juice. Lays the foundation for the day an makes sure you start your body of being alkaline. |
| Day | - Mindfullness or Guided meditation 5 - 30 Min<br>*Not every day, but if I´m on a train or just need a break it does wonders. | Always take the stairs and to the meeting if you can! | - Raw Food/Salad or anything alkaline (I do cheat days on saturday like recommended in the 4 Hour Body)<br>- Supplements (7 different kinds)<br>* Have not been ill since I start taking these in 2011 |
| Evening | - Journal 10 Min.<br>* Acknowledgements, Gratitude, Was I true to myself, Trophies, Law of Attraction, Incantation, Picture of me<br>- Reiki 30 Min. - 1 Hour or QiGong for 20 Min.<br>* I try to stay ahead of times of challenge and charge my batteries before as well as after. | - Aikido 1-2 times a week<br>* great way to boost energy and mind.<br>- Yoga/Stretching - I mix in Yoga and stretching on off days. Great way to release energy and recharge | - Light Meal<br>* Soup, Salad or fish. Your body uses a lot of energy to digest food. If you eat heavy meal late at night, you body does not rest and you feel exhausted.<br>- Supplements (7 different kinds)<br>- Drink much more water than you think you need. |

* This is my current routine. In the future it may look different, but these habits have done wonders for my life. Start with one and then add one if you feel it works.

## Your Business Has Habits Too

So how does understanding personal habits apply to your business? Well, as we've discussed, your business is a set of processes which are grouped together into a system. These processes, and the actions they involve, are repeated on a daily basis, just like your personal habits. If the processes (or habits) are the right ones, they will make money; if they're not, they won't, and they need to be changed – just like your personal habits need to be changed if they aren't the right ones for you and you aren't getting the results you want. The habits of your business and the habits of your personal life also intersect with each other – you should be designing your business to create a system that works best for you so that you can add maximum value where you are meant to do so; and you should be designing your day-to-day life to include habits that will allow you to achieve freedom while continuing to maintain your business. An example of how I've designed my habits to suit me: I don't start work until 10.30am, which is at least an hour-and-a-half after the 'normal' start of the working day. Why? Because I don't work well before then – the early morning is not my 'optimum working time'. All my life people have said, 'Erlend, you're so grumpy in the morning'. I'm not really grumpy, I'm just not in my optimum working time in the morning, so I don't like having to do things that feel like work. Instead, I meditate, I make myself a green juice, I exercise, sometimes I read ten pages of a book to help set the tone for the day – and then when I start working I'm refreshed, happy, and effective. Below, I'm going to explain some key habits that relate to your daily work life, and which will help you achieve this freedom.

# *Exercise:* Optimum Working Time

*Are you a morning person or a night person? Be honest with yourself when answering these questions:*

- *Do you jump out of bed in the morning?*
- *Do you need time in the morning to get going, i.e., are you a slow starter?*
- *When are you most in flow during the day?*
- *If you could choose your working hours, what would they be?*
- *Do you like going to bed?*

*We all have our own biological rhythms and ways of working, and we should listen carefully to these in order to maximize our efficiency. This doesn't tend to be possible if you have a normal desk job – you have to live by someone else's rhythm – but one of the great advantages of being an entrepreneur is that you set the hours, and you can finally tap into what your mind and body really needs.*

---

**Don't forget to check out my video about this exercise at**
http://youwillneverworkagain.com/exercises/

---

Before that, however, I want to mention perhaps the most important habit – which is to put aside some time on a regular basis to think about how your business system is working. You need to set aside some time to think creatively and logically about how your business is working and how the systems you are running can be improved and refined to work more efficiently. I said in chapter four that testing and refining systems is one of the most important parts of developing a new business, and that applies just as much once your business is established – there is always going to be something that can be changed or improved, or an inefficiency that can be cut, but you will never be able to identify and target these things if you don't consciously put aside some time each day to think about them. This is what we can call 'infinite loop thinking' – continuously refining things, testing them out, and then refining again to keep yourself and your business in optimal shape.

So make this the first of your habits – schedule some time in your calender for the next week to think about your business systems and how they can be improved. You want this time to be designed in the way that helps you think best. If you need to be alone to think creatively, make sure you communicate this to your employees or your family so they won't interrupt you; if you work best by bouncing your ideas off a business partner or colleague, then get that person on board as well. In theory, this time could be scheduled for once every couple of days, or even once a week, but it will work most effectively if you can put aside as little as fifteen minutes every day. This will give you the opportunity to analyze the actions of the day while they are still fresh in your mind, and will help you to ingrain this 'thinking time' as a continual habit – remember, it takes ninety days to really start up a new habit properly. It would be futile for me to suggest that you immediately block off fifteen minutes of thinking time in your daily schedule for the next ninety days, because you won't do it – but schedule that time for the next week, and see how many benefits it brings you. I'm guessing that by the end of the week it will have been useful enough that you'll be scheduling it for the week after. And then the week after that, and the one after that, and...before you know it, you've been doing it for ninety days and longer, and you have a new and incredibly useful daily habit – one that benefits you and your business.

# Exercise: *7X Brain Gym*

*Go ahead right now and schedule in at least fifteen minutes of thinking time every day for a week into your diary or calendar. If you have a business partner, employees or family that might otherwise interrupt this time, communicate to them that you need this time alone each day to improve your business (or ask them to join in if you'd like to bounce ideas off them). Now – do it! Don't forget to jot your ideas down as they come to you so you don't forget them, and remember that you'll get stronger at thinking about your business and identifying weaknesses and opportunities the more you practice doing so.*

*If you need something a little more structured to base your thinking time around, I've provided seven key questions below that I think about on a regular. You could turn them into your own 'seven day brain gym' by planning to consider one of them in each of your scheduled thinking times. Or you could just use them as guidance for designing your own questions and your own way of using the time. If you sit down and think about one of these questions deeply every day, you will start making more money.*

- *What are the biggest problems facing my customers, and how can I solve them in a way no-one else is doing?*

- *How can I streamline and minimize my business and its expenses – how can I 'cut the crap'?*

- *What mistakes have I made recently, and what can I learn from them?*

- *What have been my biggest achievements recently – am I getting closer to my long-term goals, and do I need to rethink those goals in any way?*

- *Are there things in my business that are not being measured, but which could be measured – to ensure that I know what the return on investment is for all my activities?*

- *Am I sitting too firmly in my comfort zone, and what actions can I take to push myself into the courage zone?*

- *What I am I doing that is unpleasant or time-consuming and should be done by someone else – what can I delegate or outsource?*

---

**I discuss this exercise in one of my video tutorials at**
http://youwillneverworkagain.com/exercises/

---

A quick example of how thinking time worked for me – by giving some thought to my business systems, I realized that I was spending way too much time checking and organizing invoices. Having identified the problem, I started to look for a solution, and put in place some new software that heavily automated and digitized this process. This saved me 1.5 hours a week. Doesn't sound like a lot. But think about how it compounds over time. If you're saving 1.5 hours every week, over the course of a year, that's 78 hours – that's more than three entire days to spend doing something meaningful, or even doing nothing at all.

In the rest of this chapter, I'm going to look at three of the habits that I think are most useful to cultivate if you are going to improve your business system and reduce the amount of time you need to spend working in the future. These habits are delegating, measuring, and disconnecting. This is the trinity of habits that are going to help free you to focus on yourself and your passions, rather than spending all your days tending to every little aspect of your business. To finish the chapter, I'll briefly discuss some useful time-saving software that I use to automate my businesses even further and to save me even more time.

## Delegate or Drown

The most important part of automation is building a system that works without you. Any system that relies on you performing a majority of its key tasks is going to end up making you tired, stressed, and unhappy, because you are going to be constantly fixing problems, managing crises, and generally working every hour of the day just to keep the business running. If you need to be involved in the day-to-day tasks of your business, then you own a job; instead, you should be leveraging other people's time, and aiming to own a system which is run by other people while you focus on more important things.

This means delegation, or passing the majority of your tasks on to other people. This can be a very difficult thing for entrepreneurs to do – they tend to see their business as their 'baby', and they don't really trust other people with it. But if you're going to achieve your goal of freedom, rather than being enslaved in a self-employed job, giving things up is vitally important. Delegate or drown.

A further advantage of delegation, beyond the fact that it will make your business more efficient and your life more manageable, is that it can make your company more valuable in the long term. You build a business to make money, and in John Warrillow's book *Built to Sell* he explains how a business that pivots around one key individual is worth a lot less than a business which is built on a system that can be replicated by anyone. A business which only stays afloat because of your personal talent and dedication is not a saleable asset – you're on the second or third level of entrepreneurship, and no-one wants to buy your business because after you're gone, there's a good chance it will fall apart. A business in which you are merely the owner and overseer of a system which is run on a day-to-day basis by other people is much more valuable – this is the fourth level of entrepreneurship, and people want this kind of business because it gives them a much stronger guarantee that things will continue to be profitable even after you ride into the sunset to live your life doing what you are meant to do. Remember that the big fortunes in the world were made when *selling* a business, not while *operating* a business.

If you're following what I'm suggesting, you should be putting aside a few minutes every day to think about your systems and how you can improve them. One of the best things you can do with this time is to think back over all the things you've done today and ask yourself – did I need to do that, or could I have delegated it to someone else and achieved the same results? You don't need to necessarily have a person in mind that you could delegate to – you can always find them among your current employees or hire someone else later – but you should be thinking about whether it would be at all possible for somebody else to do the work you are doing. If the answer is yes, then delegate it.

This is the big principle here – if something can be delegated, you should delegate it. Finding the right person to delegate to might require a bit of searching, but it will be worth it when you have more free time. The right person will vary depending on the scope and complexity of the task. For example, some tasks that require certain types of knowledge I delegate to my personal assistant in North America. Other things that require different skills I give to my personal assistant in the Philippines. Even small, individual tasks can be delegated to someone else through websites like Fiverr (http://fiverr.com/) if they don't involve enough work to permanently hire a new employee. And when you've delegated a task to someone else, measure how well they do to determine if you've given it to the right person..

Delegation costs money, at least at first, because you need to pay other people to do your tasks for you. This can also put new entrepreneurs off, especially considering the urge to 'cut the crap' and keep your expenses to a minimum. However, the costs of delegating are soon made up for by the extra efficiency it gives you. Take accounting for example – even if you're only a small business, you shouldn't be doing your own accounting – it takes hours and you're simply not going to be as good or as efficient at doing it as a professional accountant. More importantly, even if you could do it as well as a professional accountant, it's not something you should be focusing your time and energy on – you can delegate it, so you should. The money you have to pay the accountant is more than made up for by the extra time you've saved, time which you can devote to the activities which will help your business grow – refining your systems, uncovering new opportunities, building relationships with suppliers and fellow business owners, and so on. In this way you're paying for other people to use their time to improve your business, so that the ultimate benefits of the work come back to you. Or you can spend the free time simply enjoying your life and following your passions – and there's no price you can put on that.

Think of delegation as being related to 'wu wei' – not doing. Don't try to interfere with and control everything in life or in your business, because you're just going to wear yourself out. Instead, let things flow – delegate the work to someone else and let them get on with it. If they fail, it's not the end of the world, and you can learn from your mistakes and identify someone better to delegate the task to next time. Meanwhile, you focus on the areas that you're most suited for, where you add the most value, and where you feel the least resistance – the areas of work and life in which you feel the greatest 'flow'. Stick to that work, and delegate everything else.

## Measure

> *"What gets measured, gets managed, and what gets managed gets done."*
>
> ~Keith Cunningham

If one of your primary aims in business is to 'sharpen the saw' – that is, to continually refine your business systems – then one of the most important habits you need to build is measuring things. Measuring allows you to see what's working efficiently and what isn't, allows you to see where the strengths and the weaknesses of your current system are, and allows you to refine things accordingly. Think about your business as an aircraft. You're the pilot, and the things you're measuring are all laid out in front of you in the cockpit. The plane, like your business, should mostly move forward without the need for intervention from the pilot; but the pilot must keep track of the data he sees in front of him, and adjust the plane accordingly to make sure things continue to travel smoothly.

The advantage that you have over a pilot is that a pilot needs to take all of this very, very seriously – if he gets something wrong, hundreds of people could die. You, on the other hand, can treat it more playfully (depending on your business, of course). If you get something wrong, you lose a bit of money and start again from where you left off – and the failure can be a learning experience that makes you more effective in the future. Because the stakes are relatively low, you can think about measurement as if you were playing a game – you pick a particular parameter that you want to measure, record how well you're doing in any one week or month, and then try to devise ways to beat your 'best score'.

Almost everything is measurable, in life and in business, especially with the various apps and software programs we have access to today. You can track your sleep patterns, your calorie and nutrient intake, your exercise, your business output, the success of your marketing, and how long specific tasks take. Most of the apps or programs used for measuring and tracking are fairly easy to use, and take up very little time once they've been set up. I've listed a lot of the most useful ones at the end of the chapter.

## Disconnect

One of the things that we often hear in the media is that we're more connected than ever, and that this is a good thing for businesses, as it allows us to operate on a global scale at all times of the day and night, and from wherever we are located. To some extent this is true, but it could equally be said that in some ways we're too connected. With smartphones, tablets, and laptops we can check our emails and take calls at all hours of the day, and we never get the chance to 'switch off' like we did as recently as five or ten years ago. We end up feeling like we're permanently at work – checking emails over breakfast, before we go to bed, and so on – and this certainly does nothing to improve our quality of life on a day-to-day basis.

You need to be able to disconnect sometimes. If you're permanently wired in to your business, how can you ever feel free? The key to this is to set up a communications hierarchy – that is, delegating a lot of your communications work to other people. Remember, if it can be delegated, it should be delegated – and a lot of the emails we send and the phone calls we make each day can be passed on to others, or at least deferred for a little while. The end result of doing this is the same as with all delegation – you have more time to devote to yourself, or to the most important 20% of your business.

The principle I use for this communications hierarchy is called 'stacking'. This basically means it's quicker to set aside one time to perform a specific task, rather than repeating it multiple times throughout the day. For example, after my panic attack, I became quite a health freak and began taking various supplements to keep optimizing my health (I haven't been ill since I dramatically changed my health habits, but that's a story for another day). But it was a pain to go through five or six bottles of pills every morning, opening each of them one-by-one, taking one pill out, putting the lid back, and so on. Instead, I bought a little container with multiple compartments, and now every 14 days I fill all the compartments with one day of supplements – so all I have to do is open the compartment, and all my tablets are ready. By getting a week's worth of pills ready at once, I save five minutes every day that I would have spent opening pill bottles. As with all habits, the time saved builds up, and the benefits compound.

# Killing Email

By 'stacking up' examples of the same task, and then performing them all at once, you get things done more quickly and efficiently. This applies to your communication – if you deal with emails and phone calls as the need arises, you'll spend all day being interrupted by them. Instead, consolidate all of your communications work into a one-hour period at the same time every day, and you'll find you're much more efficient at getting it done and moving on to more important things, safe in the knowledge that you don't need to reply to another email for the rest of the day.

So, I only respond to my emails for one hour a day. If someone sends me an email five minutes after that hour is over, it has to wait until tomorrow. I've set up an autoresponse email that explains this to people as well, so that when people email me, they get an explanation of why I'm not replying to them immediately, and contact information for real emergencies. There is a double advantage to this – firstly, because I've explained that this is one of my habits and I have good reasons for doing it, people understand that I'm not being rude or ignoring them; and secondly, it trains people not to bother me with little things. After someone has emailed me a few times and received this response, they become less likely to email me with small and frivolous things – my staff will try to solve problems themselves before contacting me; and my clients and customers will be directed to the people that can help them straight away. I also sometimes add a 'frequently asked questions' section to the email, to cover common queries. And the emergency contact info? Hardly anyone ever uses it, and most people are able to determine the difference between a truly urgent situation, and one which can wait until tomorrow. An example of my autoresponder is below.

> ### *Greetings!*
> *For questions about;*
>
> *\*3sixty\* 360 Photography - <u>stiansen@3sixty.no</u>*
> <u>*Click here for FAQ on 360 Photography*</u>
>
>
> *\*3sixtyfactory\* Image Editing Services -*
> <u>*ramms@3sixtyfactory.com*</u>
> <u>*Click here for FAQ on 360 Image Editing Services*</u>
>
>
> *\*YouSpin\* 360 Software - <u>brigitte@3sixtyfactory.com</u>*
> <u>*Click here for FAQ on 360 Software*</u>

*Due to a high workload, I am currently checking and responding to emails around 1300 GMT (or your time zone). If you require urgent assistance that cannot wait until 1300 please text me on my mobile <u>+47 930 27 786</u>. Remember to include your email in your message so I can get back to you.*

*Thank you for understanding this move to more efficiency and effectiveness. It helps me accomplish more to serve you better.*

*All the best*

*Erlend*

Another thing to keep in mind when dealing with your emails is the 'If/Then' principle. Basically, when you're replying to your emails at a set time every day, make sure you save time on needless back and forth discussions and clarifications by taking a minute to say to yourself: "IF I've explained this well enough THEN the person I'm writing to will not have any further questions; IF I write in a vague way and leave things unexplained THEN I'll have more emails to respond to when they ask for clarification". With that in mind, always take a moment to read over what you have written and think about whether you can make it clearer, rather than simply hitting 'send' as soon as you're finished. Yes, it means each individual email might take a minute longer, but it will make your overall email flow much more efficient.

## One Phone Call a Day

In terms of phone calls and general work emails, they all go through my personal assistant in the Philippines. I have set up my mobile answer phone to direct people to email me, as follows:

*"Hello, this is Erlend's answer phone. The absolute best way to reach Erlend is to email him at erlend@mroutsource.com, that's erlend@mroutsource.com. (Your name) does not listen to his voice messages and therefore email is the fastest way to reach him. Have a nice day."*

This will train your clients and employees to email you instead of calling you.

This makes things even easier for me, as it weeds out the unnecessary or time-wasting messages – my PA compiles a list at the end of the day of the emails and phone calls I need to respond to and the tasks I need to undertake. She puts everything I need to know in one short email – meaning I don't have to waste time reading every little thing anyone sends to me, and I can spend more time formulating a proper reply.

# *Exercise:* Smartphone, Dumb Phone

*This is a little related exercise that I think emphasizes our over-reliance on technology and the potential downsides it has on our free time. Basically, when you first set up a communications hierarchy it can be difficult to keep away from your emails because your smartphone is always bleeping to tell you you've got mail. There's a great temptation to just have a quick look to see if it's anything important – don't fall into this trap! It's inefficient and it's wasting time that you could be spending on better things – everyone knows you're going to get back to them because you set up an autoresponder, and your PA is making a list of people you need to reply to, so you need to stop procrastinating by checking your damn phone every five minutes!*

*One way to make sure you get out of this habit is to switch back to a 'dumb phone'. Some people will recoil in horror at the idea of going backwards technologically, but really, apart from checking your emails (which you're not going to do more than once a day anymore), what value does a smartphone add to your life? Wasting time on the internet, playing games, fiddling with apps...? OK, so I'm being a bit extreme, and there are legitimately useful things that a smartphone can do, but I still think it's worth trying to go without for a week, even if only to prove that you can.*

*So this exercise is simple – just switch back to using a dumb phone for a week and see how it affects your productivity. If you get less done because you actually need the features a smartphone offers, than go back; but in a lot of cases, I think you'll find you actually get more done without the distraction. Try it and see.*

> **I talk more about this issue in a tutorial at**
> http://youwillneverworkagain.com/exercises/

## The Daily Update

Another trick is related to employees reporting to me. Rather than have my employees contacting me several times a day to tell me what they're doing, what problems they're having, what they need from me, and so on; I insist that they send me a daily update at the end of the work day. This daily email needs to include only three points:

1. What they've done today.

2. What challenges they faced.

3. What questions they have for me.

This is all the information I need to keep on top of what's happening with my businesses and to know what I have to do to keep things running smoothly – and it takes me about two minutes to read, maybe less. This is an excellent way of saving time and streamlining your communications.

# **Exercise:** *Communications Hierarchy*

*For this exercise, you need to set up your own communications hierarchy, to reduce the amount of time you spend responding to emails and phone calls. There are three steps to this, depending on the specifics of your business.*

*Step one: set up an autoresponder. This can be done however advanced your business is, and creates the good habit of only checking and replying to emails once a day. Exactly how to do it varies between email providers, but they should provide clear instructions on their help pages. As for what should be in your autoresponder – well, I've shown you mine, which you could use as your starting point, but really you can say whatever you like as long as you keep it polite and professional. The most important thing to emphasize is that their message will be responded to at some point soon, and that you are instituting this system to increase your efficiency and improve the level of service you provide.*

*Step Two: delegate communications duties. If you have a personal assistant, now is the time to give most of your communication work to them. My PA takes my calls and sifts through my email to provide me with a quick update of who I need to reply to every day, and then I get all of that done in one go. You could even ask your PA or VA to draft emails or prepare talking points for a phone call if their English is good enough. If you're looking for a VA in the Philippines with good English, we can help you with that at* hello@mroutsource.com.

*Step three: the daily update. If you have other employees besides your PA, get them to communicate with you via daily updates, rather than simply emailing you every time a problem comes up. Remember, their daily update should include three things: what they did today, what problems they encountered, and any questions they have for you. If you can get your staff into this habit, they'll be more likely to solve problems themselves rather than relying on you, and you'll be saving a considerable amount of time.*

---

**To hear more about communications hierarchies, check out**
http://youwillneverworkagain.com/exercises/

---

Before finishing this chapter with some of the useful gasgets and pieces of software I use to automate my business, don't forget that you can learn more about tips, tricks, and tools for automation with my free training videos at http://www.worklessearnmore.tv/.

## Some Useful Gadgets

- Fujitsu Scan Snap - My trustworthy scanner has been with me all over the world and I don't travel anywhere without it.

- JamBox - Mini-speaker that connects beautifully through Bluetooth. Another must-have gadget for the road.

- Kindle/iPad - Your all-in-one library and everything else tool.

- MacBook Air - Strong and sturdy hardware and software for the laptop entrepreneur that spends a lot of time traveling and in coffee shops.

## Some Useful Software

To end this chapter on automating and saving your time for more valuable things, I thought I'd briefly mention a few other pieces of software that I use to make my day more efficient and to allow me to work less.

- Screenflow (http://www.telestream.net/screenflow/) & Camtasia (http://www.techsmith.com/camtasia.html) – great pieces of recording software with which you can make videos or get screen captures. I find this very useful because it's often easier to simply explain something through speech rather than writing it down. So I record myself explaining things and either email them straight to the relevant person, or upload them to YouTube as an 'unlisted' (i.e. private) video and send the link. This could be used for dictating a blog post and getting one of your employees to transcribe it; to give demonstrations of particular processes to new employees; or to record meetings so your staff can minute them later on.

- Skitch (https://itunes.apple.com/us/app/skitch-snap.-mark-up.-share./id425955336?mt=12) – if you're often working on developing websites, and need to demonstrate small changes to your developer, this is one of the easiest ways to do it. It allows you to 'draw' on the website, circling and highlighting things that need to be changed and making it much easier for your developer to understand what you want.

- Kajabi (https://newkajabi.com/)- Easy to use online software for developing your own personal training site.

- YouTube (www.youtube.com) - For uploading and sharing video tutorials on how to do things in your business.

- Skype (www.skype.com/en/) - the free voice, chat and video conferencing software owned by Microsoft. For group video you need to be a premium member, which is a bit of a drawback, but check out Google Hangout and you can have it for free.

- Harvest (http://www.getharvest.com/) - Hour tracking software used and recommended by websites such as Guru.com. We use it to track hours at MrOutsource.com because it gives you optics on how much people work and what projects they have worked on. It's a great example of how to use cheap software to automate parts of your business, and to measure output.

- Last Pass (https://lastpass.com/misc_download.php) - A great way to securely share your passwords with people. The software also memorizes all your passwords in a secure system so you don't have to go around remembering all of them or keeping them in a Word document on Google Drive.

- Coach.me (https://itunes.apple.com/us/app/lift/id530911645?mt=8) - An app created to help you improve your daily habits. They have made the habit tracker social so you can share your habits with a group of people, and also put in stakes so you actually follow-through with them.

- Jot Not (https://itunes.apple.com/us/app/jotnot-pro-pdf-scanner-for/id307868751?mt=8) - Use your smartphone to scan and email any kind of document. The app syncs directly with popular software such as Evernote and Dropbox. Love it!

- RunKeeper (http://runkeeper.com/) - Track your exercise and get great measurements on all sorts of exciting data. Syncs with WiThings and UP, which makes it more of an all-in-one tracking system, preferable to having 10 different ones.

- Nike Fuelband (http://www.nike.com/us/en_us/c/nikeplus-fuel [http://swoo.sh/1450tkk]) - Doubles as a cool-looking watch and activity counter. You get Nike Fuel Points every day and it's easy to set a daily goal. Syncs nicely with the Nike Fuel system online, giving you a great overview of daily, weekly, monthly and yearly activity.

- UP (https://jawbone.com/up) - If I had to to choose between UP and Nike Fuelband, however, I would definitely choose UP. UP tracks your movement and sleep in a very seamless way that gives you a great overview of these two very important factors for your health. Sleep is even more important than exercise! If you don't get enough sleep you don't allow your body to heal and have enough energy to do the exercise in the first place! UP also tracks diet, but I find this part of the app a bit of a pain to use.

- Withings (www.withings.com) - Super cool gadgets for measuring weight, BMI, body fat, water percentage and $CO_2$ level in your bedroom. They also have a blood pressure device and a step counter.

- Dropbox (www.dropbox.com/) - I have all my files stored both on my laptop and in my Dropbox. A superb way of keeping everything on the cloud, giving you peace of mind in case you spill your coffee on your laptop.

- Expensify (www.expensify.com/) - A nicely developed app that allows you to track all your business expenses on the go. I personally write on my receipts, scan them and send them to my VA in the Philippines who coordinates it all with my accountant, but I have many friends that love the Expensify system.

- Carrot (www.meetcarrot.com/todo/) - The to-do list that humors and mocks you at the same time. Always gives me a daily giggle! If you like the app then check out Carrot 2, the alarm clock!

- Google Business Apps (https://apps.google.com/intx/en/) – OK, this isn't exactly news to anyone, but I still think it deserves to be here. Google's suite of applications is an incredibly useful tool for sharing and storing files as well as working collaboratively on things with employees who might be on the other side of the world. Best of all – it's affordable for even the smallest business.

- Evernote (https://evernote.com) – a really brilliant program that lets you store and organize pretty much anything that comes into your brain. You can type up notes and ideas and also save webpages and pictures, and it's all searchable afterwards. You can also sync folders across multiple devices, which can be very useful for saving time and delegating work. For example, whenever I have a travel bill, I take a quick scan of it and save it to an Evernote folder which is synced to my personal assistant's computer in the Philippines – she collects them all up, puts them in order, and sends them on to my accountant for me. Only saves me an hour or two a week, but these savings add up over a year and longer.

- Zen Desk (http://www.zendesk.com/) – this is an excellent bit of customer service software that will automate the way you and your employees deal with questions and queries. It creates an automated system which collects the relevant details of a problem, allows your employees to keep track of existing ones, and to mark them as solved when they're finished. I've been using this for the customer service side of my business, and it's never let me down.

- Time Track Pro (http://timetrack.bloop.info/) – tracks how long you spend using any particular piece of software (only for Macs at the moment).

# Resources

David Allen, *Getting Things Done: The Art of Stress-Free Productivity* (Penguin Books, 2003)

Sam Carpenter, *Work the System: The Simple Mechanics of Making More and Working Less* (Greenleaf Book Group, 2011)

Charles Duhigg, *The Power of Habit: Why We Do What We Do and How to Change* (William Heinemann, 2012)

Jeff Olson, *The Slight Edge: Turning Simple Disciplines Into Massive Success* (Success Books, 2005)

John Warrilow, *Built to Sell: Creating a Business That Can Thrive Without You* (Penguin Group, 2011)

Steven Watts, *The People's Tycoon: Henry Ford and The American Century* (Vintage, 2005)

# CHAPTER 7

# Ticket to Freedom:
## Outsourcing and Other People's Time

*"One should treat others as one
would like others to treat oneself."*

~ The Golden Rule

I talked about my own story a lot in the first chapter, and honestly, despite what you might think, I don't like talking about myself too much – I'm more interested in helping you become better entrepreneurs. Nevertheless, I want to give you another quick example from my own life. This is after I finished my first photography business in the UK and started a similar one back in Norway. It's about 6am on a weekday morning, and I'm watching the sun come up. And I'm at breaking point, mentally, but also physically. I haven't slept all night because of the work, and both of my arms are in intense pain from repetitive strain injury – doing the same thing over and over again can be really bad for you – which is just making the work take even longer. Something needs to change, I need to find a way to reduce the physical and mental burden of personally fulfilling all the orders that my company is getting. And this was the start of my journey towards outsourcing.

## What is Outsourcing?

Outsourcing is the clearest and most obvious expression of using other people's time for your own benefit. It is similar to the division of labor that Henry Ford pioneered when manufacturing cars a hundred years ago. Ford didn't spend his own time on the factory floor, putting cars together with his own hands – he followed the Pareto principle and put his efforts into building up a system of marketing and logistics (the 20%), and employed other people to do the repetitive daily tasks of actually making the product (the 80%).

The difference between outsourcing and the Fordist division of labor is the difference in how globally connected our economy and society is today. Many people describe our modern economy as post-Fordist, but I'm not so sure that's true – I think we can still build simple but efficient systems that leverage other people's time to create things of value, in the way that Ford did. The difference is that because of new communication and transport technology, our options in building that system are no longer restricted to our own geographical area – I work with people located on three different continents every day.

Ford was building big, heavy pieces of machinery, and he needed to employ people who lived near to his factories. With the business models I talked about in chapter four, the product is usually not as big and heavy as a car – it's either a purely online service (like digital music products or apps) or it's a product that can be shipped around the world relatively easily because of our modern transport technologies (as in the dropshipping business). This, combined with our ability to make free long-distance phone calls, video calls, to send emails, and to generally conduct business via the internet, means that you are not as restricted as Ford was in your choice of worker – you can hire the best person for the job at the right price, wherever they are in the world. Thomas Friedman got it right when he said that 'the world is flat' – if you need a personal assistant, then the field is no longer skewed towards people who live near to you. Instead, you can find the skills you need in someone who lives on the other side of the world, and there are almost no barriers between the two of you anymore. The best bit from the perspective of a budding entrepreneur? This freedom to search the globe for the right employee can reduce your costs massively.

Outsourcing sounds like something big and complicated, but let's be honest – you already outsource a lot of the things in your life to other professionals around you. If you feel sick, do you go to the nearest meadow and pick medicinal herbs, or do you get a doctor to look at you and determine what's wrong? If your toilet breaks, do you fix it yourself and end up making an even bigger mess all over your house, or do you hire a plumber to do the job for you? Outsourcing is no different from this – you're hiring other people to do the work for you, to make your life easier. The only difference in this case is that I'm suggesting you hire people from another country – and with communications technology as it is today, that doesn't need to be any more complicated than talking to your local doctor or plumber.

Let's get something very clear here from the start: your freedom begins with your first hire. It's impossible to run a business and have a large degree of freedom without leveraging other people's time. Whatever software you run or clever automated techniques you employ, you must have people to run and maintain those systems and techniques for you, because if it's you that's doing it you have no freedom. As you remember from the cash quadrant, employees trade their time for money – this is NOT something you should be doing as an entrepreneur!

# Why Companies Outsource

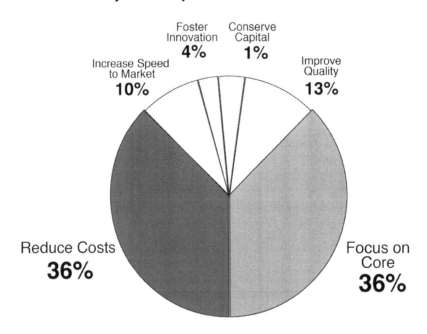

Source: (The 2001 Outsourcing World Summit)

Take a quick look at the diagram above, from the 2001 Outsourcing World Summit. Over 70% of business owners surveyed for that event said that they outsource for one of two reasons – to reduce costs, and focus on their core business. That means outsourcing allows you to 'cut the crap' as I've encouraged you to do, by keeping your expenses down; and lets you spend more of your time focusing in the core 20% that the Pareto Principle points us towards.

## NWA Work Process

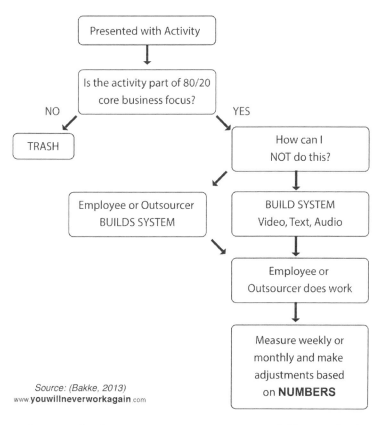

Source: (Bakke, 2013)
www.youwillneverworkagain.com

When considering whether to outsource, you can follow a fairly simple decision making process, as represented in the flow chart above. To start with, when you're presented with an activity, ask yourself whether this is a necessary part of your business focus –

your 80/20 approach to business that we've discussed previously. If it isn't, get rid of it; if it is, it's time to think about whether you can outsource it. As we know from the previous chapter, the first step is to build a system around it – work out the necessary resources and the steps that have to be taken to finish this activity. Make them as simple as possible, so they can be done by anyone you choose to outsource to. Of course, if you already have outsourced employees, you may be able to get them to do this step for you. Once you have a system in place, hire an outsourced worker, and train them to adhere to the system. Make sure you measure their progress and the success of the system, so you can identify changes that need to be made and determine whether your outsourcing is working.

Outsourcing is essentially similar to delegation – you take elements of your work that can be done by other people, and you find the people to do them. In the rest of this chapter I'm going to be discussing some of the details of outsourcing your work to other countries – particularly the Philippines – including what you should outsource, how you should organize it, and why the Philippines is my favorite place to outsource to. By the end of the chapter, you should have a pretty good idea of how to get started – but another great advantage of outsourcing is that it's cheap and you can afford to experiment with it without too many negative consequences if things go wrong. And remember, one of the key lessons of this book is that you shouldn't be afraid to fail, because failure is how we learn and improve – so I encourage you to take the lessons I'm about to give you, and jump straight in to outsourcing, learning your own lessons, and making your own mistakes in the process.

## So Why The Philippines?

Whenever people ask me questions about outsourcing, one of the main pieces of advice I always give them is that you should be outsourcing to the Philippines. People often find this a bit odd – they think to themselves, there's so many countries in the world, why not shop around a bit and find somewhere even cheaper? Of course, if you want to try outsourcing to India, Vietnam, Jamaica, Malaysia, wherever – be my guest. As I've said, outsourcing is a relatively cheap way to run a business, so if it goes wrong, you can always pick yourself up and start again somewhere else – and most of the lessons in this chapter would be applicable in those other contexts. But I strongly recommend focusing first and foremost on the Philippines, for a number of reasons:

- The cost of living in the Philippines is much lower than in North America or Western Europe, meaning that you can pay your outsourced workers a fair wage while still saving money.

- The Philippines has a lot of cultural similarities to the USA – it used to be an American colony in the first half of the twentieth century, and English remains one of their official languages. This makes Filipinos much easier to do business with than people from other countries in the area, where English is not so prevalent.

- Generally speaking, Filipinos have a decent level of education and are able to easily deal with most of the demands of any of the business blueprints I mentioned in chapter four.

- Filipinos tend to have personal qualities that make them a joy to work with – I've owned a company in the Philippines since 2008, and I have always found my employees to be honest, loyal, smart, and hard-working.

Of course, the Philippines isn't the perfect country for everything, or everyone would be hiring their employees there. There's limits to what you can get done with Filipinos, and you need to think about exactly what it is your business needs are in order to determine what you need to be looking for in employees. For example, as well as having a Filipino personal assistant, I also have another assistant in the US – I use him for tasks that require a better understanding of the Western cultural context. Equally, sometimes I need software developers, and finding people in the Philippines with the right skill level for that kind of work can be difficult. In those cases, I tend to turn to places like Croatia – it's still cheaper than working in Western Europe or the US, but Croatians are more likely to have advanced computer science educations and, as an additional benefit, they have a better understanding of the European software market than a similarly skilled Filipino might have. So you do need to put some thought into the exact requirements of any task, but for general tasks I've found that the Philippines is one of the most reliable places you can look.

## What to Outsource?

The simplest answer here is similar to the issue of what to delegate – if you can outsource something, and it would be cheaper to outsource it than to get it done domestically while still retaining a similar level of quality, then you should outsource it. To be more specific, there are a few things that I always tend to outsource to my employees in Davao City in the Philippines.

Firstly, my personal assistant, who I've already referred to several times. Her name is Regina, and she's been working with me since 2009. She knows my business inside-out at this point, and is probably the main reason that everything keeps running smoothly for me. She performs all those day-to-day tasks that are vital to the continuation of a business, but which sap your time and energy if you're a business owner – in particular, she's the one who screens my emails and phone calls and sends me a daily update with all the things I need to act on, saving me hours and hours of time. Here's one of the things about a personal assistant – you need to find the right one, and when you've found them you need to keep hold of them. It's no good having a mediocre PA because they need to be able to take on a lot of the tasks that are costing you your freedom at the moment. And when you find the right person, treat them well, pay them well, show them that they have job security, and keep them inspired and motivated – because you won't want to go back to doing this work yourself.

Another thing I tend to outsource is customer service and call center work. If you're setting up a dropshipping business (or any other kind of business), you want to have a number that customers can ring with queries, questions and complaints (though hopefully not too many of the latter), and you want to make sure that you are not on the end of that number – hopefully, you'll be selling enough items that it will be totally implausible for you to be answering every phone call anyway. The Philippines is great for this kind of work because, as I've mentioned above, due to the dominance of the US in the past political and cultural life of the Philippine, Filipinos tend to speak excellent English. This keeps your customers happy and well-served, and Filipino employees will tend to be sharp enough to work out what the problem is and address it for your customers without needing to get you involved every time. This is similarly true for work that involves communicating with other businesses, such as dropshipping – when I get an order to my dropshipping business, my employees can ensure that the company that produces the item has all the information they need and is ready to ship the product.

Two other things that I outsource to the Philippines are internet marketing (for example, search engine optimization) and web programming. These tend to require slightly more specific skills than some of the other roles, but as I've said, the standard of education in the Philippines is pretty good, and there are a lot of people with advanced skills in this kind of work who can give you a final product as good as any you'd get from Europeans or Americans. And even if you do need to put a little time, effort, and money into training your staff, I assure you that in terms of wages over the lifetime of your business, this will be totally worth it.

There are, of course, many other potential roles for outsourced workers – you just need to work out what your business needs, and then decide if the advantages and abilities of workers in places like the Philippines are a good fit for those roles. In general, I find that Filipinos are skilled enough to make it possible to outsource most things – from technical IT stuff, to social media work, to the training of other staff, and even the management of your supply chains and your company system.

# Exercise: *Three Steps to Freedom*

*Let's start with a little exercise to think about what you can and should be outsourcing from your business. Take a piece of paper and divide it into three columns. Headline the three columns with the words 'Can't Do', 'Don't Want To Do', and 'Shouldn't Do'.*

*Now, quite simply, fill the first column up with activities that need to be done in your business, but which you don't really have the technical skills to do by yourself. This could be building a website, for example, or sorting out your accounts. In the second column, list the things in your business that you don't enjoy doing – it could be answering emails or phone calls, or various kinds of administrative work, anything you can think of. Finally, in the third column, list the things that you shouldn't be doing as a business owner. This final column is a little bit trickier, as in theory it could include things that you enjoy a little bit, or at least don't mind doing. Maybe you like talking to customers on the phone – some people have that natural charm and personality that makes them good talkers. But even if you enjoy it, you shouldn't be doing it yourself, it's a job for someone much lower than you. If you want to spend all day talking on the phone, your life would be easier if you just got a job in a call center. You're a business owner now, and you need to stop doing these little day-to-day tasks that make up the 80% of less important work, so that you can focus on that optimal 20%.*

*When you're finished, you'll have a fairly comprehensive list of the things you should be outsourcing. You might not be able to give them all up immediately, but you should always be aiming to get these tasks off your personal to-do list as quickly as possible. Read the rest of the chapter to get some inspiration, and then get going!*

> **Check out my tutorial for this exercise at**
> http://youwillneverworkagain.com/exercises/

## How to Organize Your Outsourcing

Now for the details – how do I actually set my system up for outsourcing? How do I leverage other people's time in the most effective manner for both me and them? There's a whole number of different elements to this, all of them learned through trial and error, and in this segment I'm going to try and explain as many of them as I can.

## The Rule of Four

If you've ever looked around you at a house party or a dinner party, you'll notice there's something special about the number four. If you have four people together in a group, all of them can follow and take part in the same conversation easily. Once you go above that number, the conversation splits – three people follow one conversation, two people follow another one. Four is the optimal number of people to ensure clear and coherent lines of communication. In a rather different context, you'll also find that many of the best jazz bands have four people in them, because this is the optimal number for the musicians to work together and stay in time during complex compositions. Consequently, I try to set my business up in a similar way – with groups of four.

# The Rule of 4

**Must Have COMPANY STRUCTURE**

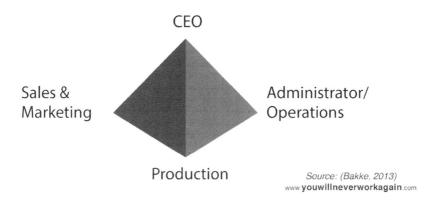

CEO

Sales & Marketing

Administrator/ Operations

Production

Source: (Bakke, 2013)
www.youwillneverworkagain.com

I make the most competent people into CEOs of the companies I own. As you can see on the diagram, these people are at the top of the pyramid of my outsourced businesses, and they report directly to me. Each of these CEOs is in charge of three managers – one for sales and marketing, one for production, and one for operations, the three main areas you should be spending your revenue on. If necessary, these people can then be responsible for up to three other people, and so on. So everyone, has three people reporting to them, making a maximum of four people in each conversation.

"But wait a minute Erlend," you may be thinking, "a pyramid actually has four corners touching the ground, but one of them is out of sight when you look at it from the front." Well spotted, eagle-eyed reader! The fourth corner hiding at the back of the pyramid is where I come in as the business owner. I'm not really visible in the everyday actions of the CEOs or the people that work beneath them, but I still have a vital role of oversight which helps to keep the whole edifice standing – after all, if you took out that invisible fourth corner, the pyramid would fall flat over.

To perform that oversight role, I simply have the CEO of each company report directly to me once a day in an email that takes me three minutes to reply to. Apart from that, we only need to communicate in emergency situations. This is how I've built my management structure, and even if you're running a particularly large and complex operation, it's easy to see how more levels can be added – the managers at the top are in charge of up to three sub-managers on the level below, each of whom is in charge of three workers, and so on.

In this way, while still keeping costs relatively low because you're hiring in the Philippines, you can spread the work out among several employees rather than overloading the one or two people you could afford for the same price in North America or Western Europe – even paying a decent Filipino wage, you're still going to be paying only around one-twentieth or less of the amount that you'd pay domestically for the same job, and as an added bonus, you'll get a surprising amount of respect. When I first started outsourcing to the Philippines, my employees would always call me 'Sir'. This seemed a little odd to me, as I was living in my parents' basement at the time, so I didn't really think of myself as someone who commanded that level of respect. So one day I said to them, "you don't need to call me Sir all the time, you know – you can just call me Erlend". But they told me in reply "we will call you whatever you want, but we prefer to call you Sir, if that's OK with you Sir Erlend!". When was the last time you hired somebody in the west and they called you Sir voluntarily? Each worker takes on a few relatively simple tasks like arranging logistics with my dropshipping partner, ensuring orders are fulfilled, dealing with customer inquiries, and keeping me up-to-date with what's going on. And because of the rule of four, communication remains clear and manageable.

## Where to Hire and When to Fire

My first employee was Rimmon. When I hired him, he was flat broke and basically lived on the street with his wife and children. He had to do his job hunting every day from a little internet cafe in Davao City. He found my advert on an employment website in the Philippines, www.sulit.ph, and applied to try out. This was for my photography and image editing business, and I was looking for people with excellent skills in photo editing, so I hired him and four other people for one month. I created short videos using screen capturing software and a microphone, in which I explained the tasks I wanted them to do, and put them on YouTube for easy viewing. I sent all five of them the same tasks for a month (and paid them for their work, of course – whereas in a lot of freelance work in the West there's sometimes an assumption that someone should do a 'test' before being hired, this isn't really fair in the Philippines, when the work is so affordable and the people need the money much more than you do). The worker who did best, despite living on the street and working from this internet cafe, was Rimmon. So I hired him full time. Now he lives in a decent house, drives a nice car, and we've worked together for many years – and I trust him so much and I know he has such an amount of natural talent that he's now my business partner.

The purpose of that little story is twofold. On the one hand, it gives you an example of how I used test exercises to weed out the weaker applicants and encourage the stronger ones, and how it's perfectly possible and affordable to do this very rigorously in the Philippines – I paid all five of my potential employees for a month's work, but in the end I've saved money on hiring and firing the wrong people, and ended up with a guy who has since rewarded my faith in him.

On the other hand, it tells you that websites like Sulit are excellent places to find diligent, talented workers.

Some of the other sites I've used in the past to find outsourced workers include eLance (www.elance.com), Guru (www.guru.com), Craigslist (www.craigslist.org) and OnlineJobs (www.onlinejobs.ph). Some of these sites don't always have the best reputation in the West, as it can be tough to find real talent on them – but it is there if you look hard enough. Equally, people find it difficult to go through all the stages of hiring their own employees – finding them, interviewing, testing, screening, training, and so on. As an alternative, you could use recruitment agencies instead – these provide staff who have been pre-screened for reliability and trustworthiness, and who have been trained in some of the main skills an outsourced business needs. I happen to run such an agency myself, so if you'd like to skip the difficult part of hiring staff, and go straight to having a dedicated, hard-working team, check it out at http://mroutsource.com/. We've already put in the work to find the cream of the crop, so you can sit back and relax as they take your business to a new level. In fact, if you turn to the back of the book, we're offering a whole range of bonus gifts and offers, including:

- Free online training for your Virtual Assistant, www.mroutsourceuniversity.com/fe/43876-mr-outsource-university-free-training

- A free ebook, *Outsourcing Mastery: 17 Secrets on How to Outsource to the Philippines,* http://youwillneverworkagain.com/outsourcing_mastery/

- 30% off recruitment services with MrOutsource.com, using the code YWNWA.

What should you be looking for in potential hires? A few things:

- First, look at the skills they bring to the table. If you need a web developer, it's more cost-effective to hire someone who costs more money but already has those skills than to try and save on wages but end up paying for training or having a poor quality website.

- Second, look for examples of past work and concrete experience – in some cases, for example, you'll end up with people telling you they're a graphic designer when really they just took a Photoshop course at college. So ask for examples of their work and experience, and if you can't find anyone with the right examples, don't be afraid to ask people to do a test sample for you – just give them some realistic instructions for the kind of work you want them to do, and see how they get on.

- Third, ask for references from previous employers or other trustworthy people – if they can provide these, they should give you a good idea of their skills level and how hard-working they are.

- Fourth, look for someone with good English – most Filipinos can speak English, but some are much easier to communicate with than others, which can be an important factor in making sure things get done in the right way. Of course, this last point counts double if you're hiring people to write articles, do SEO work, or deal with customers from your own country.

- And finally, ask them to send you a video of themselves where they explain why they want to work for you, what motivates them, why they love what they do and where they want to be in five years time. You can alter these questions to be more specific to your business, but try to find out their true passions and purpose and see if they are aligned with what you can offer them. By asking them for more than just their normal CV you get to test how much they want the job, and you weed out the lazy ones early in the process.

A quick note on firing people – it's always best to get rid of bad performers as quickly as possible, and I suggest 'recycling' the worst performing employees to strengthen your team. The mantra 'how you do anything is how you do everything' is a very true one, and if you have an employee who gives little attention to his work or turns up late, they're only going to get worse rather than better – so get rid of them. I had a web designer who I knew was pretty incompetent, but he only had one simple job – to make regular back ups of our websites – so I kept him on, thinking that he surely couldn't mess that up, and it was easier than hiring someone new. Big mistake. He didn't make the back ups, we got hacked, and we lost $20,000 of websites in one go, and all because I should have fired this guy and replaced him with someone better. I don't make that mistake anymore.

How do I find a good replacement for people I fire? I go to my top performing employee and I ask if they know anyone they could recommend. They always do, and that person is always a good worker as well – you are defined by the four or five people you spend the most time with, so in general, negative people hang out with other negative people, and positive people hang out with other positive people. As the old saying goes, "birds of a feather flock together" - so your top employees are going to know people who can be your future top employees. Get rid of your worst performers, and bring in these guys.

## Training

This is likely not the first self-growth book you are reading. Maybe you have a bunch of information products on your shelf? eBay trading, secrets of real estate investing, and so on? Give these to your first employee, and get them to start implementing the systems and tricks from those products for you. You shouldn't be the one watching 400 million video tutorials on how to execute the strategy. True entrepreneurs get other people to do the work for them, remember. I spend a lot of money on high quality info products and give them to my employees to implement. I want the benefit of the learning, but I have no big interest in becoming an expert at whatever each particular info product may be about. Your ticket to freedom is getting other people to learn the things you need to have done, then you let them do it for you, and the chances of your success dramatically increase.

You might be tempted to try and skip training expenses, but I want you to remember another old saying – if you give a man a fish he eats for a day, if you teach a man to fish he eats for life. With the amount of benefits you're going to be getting from your outsourced staff, it's only fair that you give them the skills they need to succeed throughout the rest of their life – so that even if your business is long gone, they'll still be able to find work for other budding entrepreneurs. Think of this as paying it forward – by providing benefits to your staff and advantages to entrepreneurs who might hire them in the future, the positive energy will eventually come back to you because of the value you've created in the world. In addition to this, you'll have workers who are better at their jobs (meaning less hassle and less costs to you for cleaning up a mess), and workers who are more loyal to you because of the valuable skills you've shared with them. Of course, if you're looking for employees who have already been trained to the highest standard, my Mr Outsource business (http://www.mroutsourceuniversity.

com/fe/43913-mr-outsource-applicants-sign-up) can provide exactly that at a low cost, allowing you to put your focus elsewhere. Or you can cash in on the free bonus we're offering to train your employees at http://www.mroutsourceuniversity.com/fe/43876-mr-outsource-university-free-training.

Related to the concept of training is that of the personality test. By personality testing both yourself and your key employees (such as the outsourced CEOs of your businesses) you can identify weaknesses and focus on improving them. Below you can see a diagram of a personality test I've used on my staff before, the Talent Dynamics test (http://talent-dynamics.com/profile-test/). Around the edge of the diagram we can see various characteristics that your workers might have – they could be creative types, supporters who help others achieve their aims, dealmakers who are useful for keeping work organized among your staff, and so on. It's impossible for one person to be equally adept at all these roles, as you can see from my profile in the middle – I got particularly good scores as a creator and a mechanic, but poorer scores as a trader and supporter. But that's fine – what you need to aim for is a good balance of these qualities across your whole team – and as you can see, the collective scores of my Filipino dream team are much more well-rounded, with equally good scores on almost all categories.

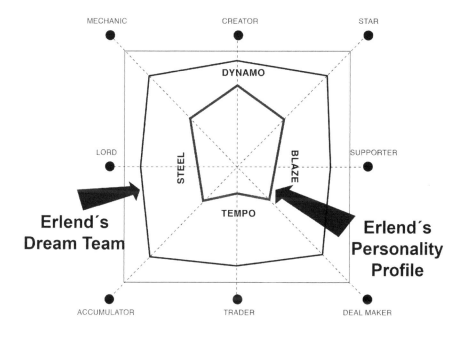

Source: *Talent Dynamic Test Erlend Bakke 2013*
www.**youwillneverworkagain**.com

Taking a personality test with your staff can be an excellent way of working out what holes may need to be filled in your organization. You might discover that you need to encourage more creativity, or help your staff work together more coherently. But as I've said before, until you measure these things in this manner, you'll never know. It's much better to take a test and consciously direct your training in this way, rather than to just blindly move forward.

## Payment

If you've never worked with Filipinos before, you're probably wondering what wages you should expect to pay. As I've said before, I pay all my workers a fair wage, and you should too – it makes them happier, healthier and more productive, and, quite simply, it's fair. You're going to be making money from their work, so it's only fair that they should make decent money for helping you. I pay my workers a starting wage of $300 a month, rising quickly to $500 a month if they prove to be good, capable workers – this is a very good wage in the Philippines, it's more than call center workers get, and working in a call center is actually considered a pretty good job in the Philippines. By doing this, I get talented hard workers with skills – which is what I want for my businesses. If you actually ask your employees what they expect to be paid, they'll quite likely say a number lower than this because most Filipinos are shy – this is a good sign, as it shows they want the work, but don't take advantage of their good nature and actually pay them too-low wages. Offer them a proper salary instead, and they'll be even more grateful to you and willing to work hard.

If a worker has a good month, I sometimes give them a bonus of around $100 – doesn't take much out of my profits, but it adds 20% to their salary, and keeps them motivated. Don't do it every month, but when they have a particularly good month it's nice to reward them.

And here's one more little tip which you'll thank me for later – in the Philippines, workers get paid a '13th month bonus'. That is, at the end of each year, you give them a bonus of a month's pay. 'Bonus' is a bit of a misleading term here, as it makes it sound like something you have discretion over – whereas in reality, it's essentially compulsory because of the hassle you'll face if you don't pay it. Most people don't realize this when they start working with Filipinos, and it can lead to problems when they don't pay it – a few of the workers will be offended that you haven't followed the custom, but more likely, the majority will be quite upset, and will assume that you didn't like their work this year. So now you know – unless someone has been really terrible at work (in which case, you should be recycling them and replacing them with someone the top performer recommends) you should pay a 13th month bonus.

Obviously, since you're unlikely to be based permanently in the Philippines yourself, you'll often be paying your people at a distance. As with communication technology, however, banking and money transfer technology is really well-developed these days, so this doesn't really pose a problem. Here are some of the websites I use to send money to my workers in the Philippines:

- Western Union (www.westernunion.com) – they will charge a large fee for transferring money to the Philippines, so it's your most expensive option – but it's also the fastest and easiest. In the Philippines there are Western Union signs everywhere because of the millions of Filipinos that live abroad and send money back home. This was the first payment method I used when I started outsourcing.
- Xoom (www.xoom.com) – this is my medium of choice, because it's fast, easy and cheap. It does have a tendency to crash occasionally or to have other minor problems which can stop you sending money, so it's good to have an account with one of the other websites as well, just as a backup. Xoom is really easy to use (as are all of these suggestions), so head over to the website and just look around – you'll get to grips with it in no time.
- PayPal (www.paypal.com) – very well-known and used across the world, but the fees tend to be a bit higher than Xoom, and it operates more slowly. A good back up option, as it's fairly reliable.
- MoneyGram (www.moneygram.com) – this is run by Walmart in the US, which means it's reliable and available in a wide range of locations in the Philippines. You wire the money, and your workers can pick it up from various places – they'll know what to do and where to go, as this is a common way of remitting money back home by Filipino workers in other countries.

- RemitHome ([www.remithome.com](www.remithome.com)) – I must admit that I haven't personally used this service yet, but it looks cheap and easy to work, so it may be worth a go if you have problems with any of the other three.

## Avoiding Problems

> *"Hope for the best, plan for the worst"*
>
> ~Lee Child

Obviously I can't help you with specific problems that come about in your line of work, because they'll be different every time – just remember what I've said before, that making mistakes is the way we learn and failure actually makes us stronger as long as we understand why we failed. What's important in this chapter is how to avoid problems in your relationship with your outsourced staff. Most of these problems are going to fall into two categories – communication and expectations. Most people are not happy because they set the wrong expectations. If you start a business and expect to always have perfectly loyal staff, clients that always pay on time, and that everyone will love your product or service, then you're setting yourself up for failure. What I do is set lower expectations and goals so I can actually be sure of achieving them and I don't get angry when things go wrong because, well, I'm expecting it.

In terms of communication, the solution is easy – set up  a daily communication system as discussed above. Particularly at the beginning of your business, there will be times when your new employees will have problems and need help. You don't want them to be contacting you all day every day, and you do want them to try and fix the problems themselves before bothering you – but you do need to know that there is or was a problem, and the steps they took to solve it, to ensure that they're actually getting it right. That's why you get your staff to send you the daily update telling you what they did today, what problems they faced, and any questions they have for you. This takes two minutes to read, and perhaps a little longer to respond to if necessary, and it leads to clear, effective communication and flags up problems early before they become too entrenched to solve easily.

Expectations can be more of a problem. This is a kind of cultural thing in the Philippines – everyone here wants to do their work perfectly, and they're all very worried that they're not doing a good enough job. Even someone who has been doing great work for you for quite a while might suddenly decide that they got one thing wrong, and now they're too embarrassed to talk to you – while to you it seems like a minor problem, to them it seems like a disaster. You can even have people who will completely disappear from contact for a while rather than face the embarrassment of explaining that they did something wrong.

So it's important to be very clear about what your expectations are from the start – how much work do you expect them to do every week, what should they do if they have a problem they can't solve, and so on. Be realistic about productivity, because if you expect too much from them and they're unable to deliver, you can easily run into the kind of problems I just mentioned, of people completely disappearing out of embarrassment. This means, of course, that you will need to make it clear that you're available to help them if they need it – this seems initially to be against the concept of 'never working again', as you might be worried that you'll be constantly sorting out problems for your employees. But it's actually quite simple – just make sure they understand that while you're around to help, you're not around 24/7 – instead, they can contact you at the end of the day and you'll help them when you respond to your emails tomorrow. Create the expectation that problems do not always need to be solved immediately, and that they should try to solve any problems that come their way while also remembering that you're there to help if they can't figure out the solution themselves.

## Trust Your Employees

My employees, who all live in a developing country thousands of miles away from my home, have access to my PayPal account, which is linked to my bank account. Even with the security measures in place to stop hackers draining my account, I still keep between $2-5,000 in that PayPal account at any one time. A lot of people would tell you I'm completely mad to give such open access to people who are relatively poor compared to me – the assumption is that poor foreigners will obviously steal from the wealthy European if they have a chance. I've never had a penny go missing. Not a single penny has ever been stolen from my well-stocked PayPal account by any of my employees.

This is because I have built up trust with my employees and I have built up relationships with them. And this saves me time that I can spend on my personal goals, on following my path – if I didn't have this level of trust, I'd be spending half my time authorizing and paying off every small bill or expense that comes through my companies. Instead, for anything under $300, my staff are authorized to process the payment via my PayPal account without having to pass it by me first (and then obviously it shows up on the accounts at the end of each month for me to quickly check over). Anything bigger than that I ask them to pass by me first, and then I let them get on with it.

This is something that many people who want to outsource their work have problems with – they don't want to or can't seem to build trusting relationships with their employees. They see their employees as simply cheap bodies who will get the work done without any of the pesky problems of European or American workers like 'wages', 'rights', or 'opinions'. This is the kind of outsourcing that gives the whole enterprise a bad press – the 'race to the bottom', where outsourcing is simply a means of getting things done as cheaply as possible. If you really want to free up your time *and* make money, rather than just making money while still being enslaved to your business, you need to build up trust and treat your employees like human beings, even when they're based on the other side of the planet. Meet them face-to-face if possible, or at least over Skype if you can't make it out to the Philippines yet, and make sure that they understand that they're a valued member of the team and you're not going to fire them without reason one day – by giving them the feeling of security and trust, you'll find that they're willing to work much harder for you, and will eventually become just as trusted to you as my employees are to me.

## The Golden Rule

This links to the above, and should really go without saying, but if you're going to take advantage of the many benefits that outsourcing to the Philippines can bring to your business, make sure that your employees get a share in some of those benefits. Don't lowball them on wages just because you think they're desperate for a job – you're already paying much less than you would if you hired at home, so at least pay them a wage that lets them live comfortably in the Philippines. Give them a bit of time off when they need it – you're trying to create freedom for yourself by leveraging other people's time, but those other people still have their own commitments, including family and friends, that they want to attend to as well. Hire them on longer-term contracts once they've proved themselves reliable, rather than keeping them on a succession of short-term contracts. Obviously you want to retain some degree of flexibility in case things change for your business or go downhill, but by providing your workers with the sense of security that a longer-term contract can give them, you'll end up with better, more reliable and more industrious workers anyway – meaning everyone benefits. Again, I shouldn't need to say this, but sometimes you have to make things very obvious before people realize them – Filipinos are your equals, and they deserve to be treated as humans, rather than simply as economic units. Yes, they're cheaper to hire than workers in your home country, but that doesn't make them disposable or less worthy of your respect. Keep that in mind when you're putting your outsourcing plan together.

## *Exercise:* Jump Into Outsourcing

*It's time to stop talking and start doing! At the beginning of this chapter we had an exercise where you wrote down all the things that you could outsource from your business – if you haven't done it yet, go back to it now. Once you have that list, pick one thing from it – a task that is fairly small, such as getting a logo designed or having the text for your website home page written. Now, it's time to go on your first outsourcing adventure. Go to one of the websites listed below where you can find freelancers and contract workers – for this kind of one-off work, I'd suggest Fiverr – look around, and hire someone to do this for you. If it goes right (and there's a very good chance it will), you'll have taken your first step towards freedom. If it goes badly for some reason, you'll only have lost $5, and you'll be able to gain some insight into what went wrong and how to avoid it next time. So don't delay! A journey of a thousand miles begins with a single step, remember, so take that first step today.*

Don't forget, if you're looking to find out even more about outsourcing, everything I couldn't fit in this chapter is available in my first book *Outsourcing Mastery: 17 Secrets For Outsourcing to the Philippines.* And I'm giving a free copy to all readers of *Never Work Again*! Just go to

http://youwillneverworkagain.com/outsourcing_mastery/.

## Resources

Robert B. Cialdini, *Influence: The Psychology of Persuasion* (HarperCollins, 2007)

Chris C. Ducker, *The Definitive Guide to Outsourcing to the Philippines* (Chris Ducker, 2012)

Thomas L. Friedman, *The World is Flat 3.0: A Brief History of the Twenty-first Century* (Picador, 2007)

Daniel H. Pink, *Drive: The Surprising Truth About What Motivates Us* (Riverhead Books, 2009)

Geshe Michael Roach, Larna Christine McNally and Michael Gordon, *Karmic Management: What Goes Around Comes Around in Your Business and Your Life* (Harmony, 2009)

## Links

You can hire people from all over the world doing micro-arbitrage, part-time, full-time or freelance on these websites.

www.Elance.com
www.onlinejobs.ph
www.upwork.com
www.Freelancer.com
www.Guru.com
www.ContentDivas.com
www.MrOutsource.com
www.Zirtual.com
www.PeoplePerHour.com
www.TaskRabbit.com
www.Fiverr.com
www.Craigslist.com

# CHAPTER 8

# Never Work Again

*"The journey is what brings us happiness, not the destination."*

~ Dan Millman,
Way of the Peaceful Warrior

So here we are at the end. Or is it the beginning? If you've been reading thoroughly and doing the exercises, you should by this point have powerful tools to start your own business or put your existing business on autopilot so that you never need to work another day. When you find your flow and get up to that fourth level of entrepreneurship, you'll find that even the tasks you have to do are no longer 'work' – because you're doing things that you love.

You'll also find that you feel more satisfied with your newfound freedom because of the entrepreneurial thinking and hard work that preceded it. The diagram below has two axes – one that goes between money you earned and money you were given, and one that goes between 'me thinking' and 'we thinking'. I can tell you from experience, both my own and that of others like the millionaire friend that I discussed earlier on, that you get considerably more happiness and fulfillment from knowing that you earned your money through hard work, and from creating value for others in the work that you do. While I hope that one day soon you'll be able to say that you're never going to work again, in the meantime I encourage you to put in the utmost effort and aim to be on the happy and fulfilled side of the line when your wealth and success finally comes.

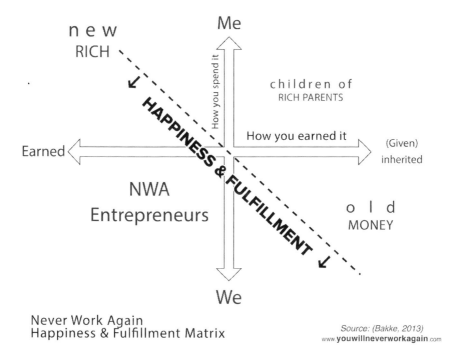

Never Work Again
Happiness & Fulfillment Matrix

Source: (Bakke, 2013)
www.youwillneverworkagain.com

## Looking Back

So what have we learned over the last few hundred pages? If I've done my job correctly, you will have learned some useful practical lessons about how to create a business, how to automate it, and how to outsource your work to others. But looking back on the text, I think three other points stand out.

The first is the need to 'cut the crap', to eliminate distractions and unnecessary expenses. This could lead you to very concrete actions – cutting out bills and subscriptions that you don't need, selling stuff you've accumulated over the years that you're never going to use, and so on. But it's more about a change of mindset – in the future, instead of listening to your impulses and your socially programmed wants, you should start thinking more consciously about what you need to make you happy in this world. In terms of money, you should be doing more with less; but you should also

223

think about how you spend an even more valuable commodity – your time. Remember, you can make more money, but you can't make more time, so use it wisely. Cut out the things that are taking up your time without making you happy, like watching TV or browsing Facebook, and concentrate your time on improving your business and spending time with the people and activities you love.

The second point is the need for focus. You should be working out what you're best at, and focusing on it like a laser. Measure everything, evaluate what is working well and what isn't, and eliminate aspects of your business that are superfluous – they are taking away time and money from the more successful parts of your work that are producing profit and can be scaled up to produce more.

The third point is the need for consistency. Remember, it takes time to build new habits, and even longer to start seeing the real effects of those habits, but it's important to do so. Think about an example from your personal life – if you're going to take up running you need to stick with it for ninety days before you really ingrain the habit. You need to wait even longer before you really start to see the benefits of a healthier heart and stronger muscles – but when it happens you realize that it was worth the effort. The same goes for your business. There might be times when you feel like you're getting nowhere, but you must keep going – it's only consistency over a long period of time that is going to lead to you becoming successful and gaining your freedom to never work again.

# How To Build Wealth & Freedom

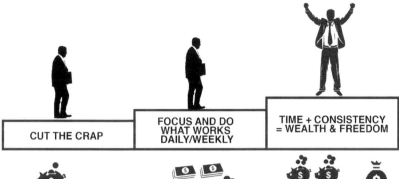

| CUT THE CRAP | FOCUS AND DO WHAT WORKS DAILY/WEEKLY | TIME + CONSISTENCY = WEALTH & FREEDOM |
|---|---|---|

## 1. ELIMINATE
- Eliminate Waste - Fees, Subscriptions, Etc.
- Simplify Your Life by Doing More With Less
- Measure & Automate Spending
- Repair Instead Of Replace
- Sell Your Unused Stuff
- Only Spend Time With Great People
- Go On A Media Diet
- Only Spend Time and Money On People and Things That Bring You Wealth and Freedom

## 2. FOCUS
- Use Other People Time
- Education/ Training in Focus Area
- Reinvest Money Into Business
- Consistently Evaluate What Works
- Innovate Only In Focus Area
- Measure Everything
- Consistently Eliminate and Get More Focused

## 3. STAY ON PATH
- Love The Compound Effect
- Keep & Improve Habits That Work
- Delegate & Build Systems
- Do More Passive Investing

*Source: (Bakke, 2013)*
www.**youwillneverworkagain**.com

Along with these three points, I've also emphasized a series of steps that I think make up a 'Never Work Again Formula'.

Step one is to 'know thyself', and where you truly are in your life process. As Jay-Z said, "knowing who you really are is the foundation of everything great".

Step two is to ask yourself the all-important questions – what is your purpose in life? What do you truly love to do? And what is your true path?

Step three is to take one of our freedom business blueprints, and the techniques of automation and outsourcing that we discussed, and apply them to the things you love. Leverage other people's time to build a business that makes you money while giving you free time to focus on the other elements you also love, and which you need to live a balanced and rich life.

And step four, which is the real profit of the philosophy – a true feeling of freedom, because you'll be always going towards what you love, doing the things that you love doing, and spending time with the people you love. You'll be living out your purpose in life, following your path, and growing as a person.

Before I sign off, I want to make a few closing remarks about some of the elements of the Never Work Again philosophy – to show you that love, growth, and freedom are all one.

Source: (Bakke, 2013)
www.**youwillneverworkagain**.com

## Love is Freedom

Freedom is doing the things you love, not the things that people tell you that you have to do, or the things that people tell you that you should love. Freedom is identifying your true passions and going towards them, so that even when most other people would look at your life and say that you seem very busy, you don't feel busy – you feel like you're enjoying your time, because you're focusing on the things you love to do. You'll find that when you do what you love for a living, and you fill up your time with your passions and interests, you really will feel like you're never going to have to work again.

More than just that, freedom is to go with the flow, as the Taoists would say; and to follow your heart, not your intellectual mind. Your intellect does a lot of good things for you, and you can't exist without it. Your intellect is great at helping you to start new, beneficial habits, but it can also be very good at trapping you into less positive ways of thinking, less useful habits, and desires for things you don't really need. The mind is like a computer program, it's great at performing logical functions and thinking through problems, but it can't tell you what you really want from life or your true purpose. For that, the heart needs to take over – that's where the truth is located. So don't think things through too much all the time – listen to your heart, and let it guide you towards what you love, and then let the mind do what it does best only once you're sure you're on the right path – the path towards your freedom.

## Freedom is Growth

In *The Road Less Traveled*, M. Scott Peck says "I define love thus: the will to extend one's self for the purpose of nurturing one's own or another's spiritual growth". So doing the things you love and living your freedom has another advantage – it leads to personal growth. Think back to the start of the book, when I told you the story of the Buddha. Which version of Prince Siddhartha had more personal growth – the one that started the story with all the material wealth he could ever want, and who followed a path of princeliness laid out for him by others? Or Siddhartha when he was the Buddha, who had understood his true purpose in life, his calling, the path he was to follow until his death?

The same principle applies in your life – love, freedom, and growth are the same thing. When you find what you love, you'll be free; and when you're free, you'll grow as a person; and as you grow, your feeling of freedom and your drive to go towards what you love will only increase. If you're experiencing all this while being a businessman and entrepreneur as well, you'll discover another interesting fact that I mentioned earlier – that entrepreneurs are actually very altruistic. Entrepreneurs are working on things that they love, which means they have a lot of freedom and a lot of space for personal growth. And this means they can develop 'we' thinking (from the heart), which replaces the old, programmed 'me' thinking (from the mind) that the majority of people have. Entrepreneurs, as people who have grown personally, have a lot of trust and faith in the good side of humanity – they know that they want to add value in the world and make it a better place for everyone, and they believe that other people want to do the same. So they help other people through their innovations, their businesses, their philanthropy, knowing that all of this value they put into the world will come back to them eventually; and this makes them happy and fulfilled, while the people focusing on the old 'me' thinking remain unhappy, unfulfilled, and depressed. And that's why true entrepreneurs are rich – it's not because they craved after money, it's because they did the exact opposite. Their wealth is a natural outgrowth of their altruistic behavior, and their 'we, not me' mindset. And this can work for you too.

When you have freedom, you'll have growth. You'll have time to grow emotionally by spending time with your family and your friends; time to grow intellectually through reading, study and critical thinking; and time to grow in understanding through traveling and undertaking new experiences. And your life will turn into a true adventure.

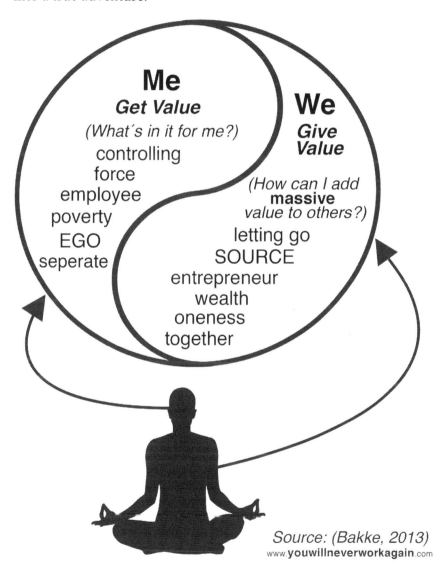

Source: (Bakke, 2013)
www.youwillneverworkagain.com

## The Path

> *"Be who you are and say what you feel, because those who mind don't matter, and those who matter don't mind."*
>
> ~Bernard M. Baruch

So now that you have all the knowledge that this book has to offer – all of the things I wish I'd known when I was making mistakes as a new entrepreneur – what are you going to do with it? Are you going to continue down the same path as before – tired, enslaved by your job or your business, dreaming of being free but never daring to actually take that first step towards real freedom? Or are you going to make changes, leverage other people's time through automation and outsourcing, and make the switch from being a wantrepreneur, a solopreneur, or an operator, to being a business owner?

If you've made it here to the end of the book, you should have some idea of what your path is, and whether it involves owning your own business. The most important thing from now on is perseverance and willpower. Sticking to your path is going to be tough at times – there's going to be the temptation to go back to your old way of life, and there are going to be people who are going to try and knock you off track. Ignore them. These challenges are just opportunities to grow. You know what you want, what you need, and what you truly desire.

You've now become aware of your programming, the habits you've formed, and the existence of your ego, and you can start to look deeper within yourself. You can stop reacting blindly to things, and start exploring where they come from and who you truly are; and you can co-exist with your ego, understanding its impulses and choosing how to respond to them – you may even occasionally be able to surrender the ego and feel truly in the flow. Some people will react to you strongly when you make these changes – some positive, some negative. Sometimes you'll have to set people straight, but that's ok – in the past, monks were often Shaolin warriors as well, so there's nothing wrong with showing strength and fighting back against people even while trying to live a life of love. Those people need the encouragement to find their own true path, and their strong reaction to you can be the first step on that journey – it's your duty to help them get there, to 'be their karma'. The most important thing among all this is to make sure you stick to your own path, no matter how difficult it may seem sometimes.

The programming you received in school, from your parents, and from society means nothing now, you can throw it off and start again with a new mindset; you can co-exist with the ego and its cravings and insecurities; the wishes of others mean nothing, except where you're aiming to add value to their lives. Just live for the moment, in the moment, and become who you really are.

I wish all of you the very best of luck on your path, whether in business or in life – although really the two are intimately connected. I look forward to working with you one day at one of my seminars, webinars, or even in one-on-one coaching – head over to the dedicated website for this book at http://youwillnever workagain.com/ for more information on all of this, as well as a collection of interviews, videos, blueprints, and more. If you enjoyed this book and would like to leave a review for it on Amazon, it would mean the world to me – and please, be as honest as you'd like, I read all the reviews and I welcome criticism as much as praise, as it helps me to make future editions of *Never Work Again* even stronger.

Thank you once more for reading – now put the book down, and go out and take that first step towards freedom.

# Free Book Guide

*So, what do you think... Are you ready?*

*Get all of the resources mentioned and much more (it's all FREE!) at the link below so that you can get started and create the lifestyle business of your dreams:*

**YouWillNeverWorkAgain.com/bonus**

# Acknowledgements

To my mother, father, and brother for supporting me in pursuing my path in life and for the love you have always given me. Christina, you are my angel. When I met you everything in my life changed for the better and you helped me find my freedom and understanding what true love really means.

Rimmon Pancito & Stian Johansen for being amazing business partners, a true joy and motivation to work with. Regina Evangelista for keeping me in line, making things happen, as well as great conversations. A big thanks to the whole team in Norway, Croatia, and the Philippines for producing great work for our clients!

Mentors, Coaches and Friends (influences from 2007 and beyond):

Simon Myers - For firing me and starting me on my true path

James Perowne - Getting me started as an entrepreneur

Keith Peavy - Light in the darkness

Jens Andreas Huseby - Believing in crazy ideas that have come true

Tim Ferriss - You changed my life

Pedro Matos - Cycling and great talks

Rick Salmon - Believing in me

Eirik Kvisli - Free office space

Tor Arne Hove - Meditation, Zen Habits, and Taoism

Cindy Rold - Teaching me success habits

Frederic Rivelsrud - For epic world travels

Keith Cunningham - Teaching me business sense

Jakob Løvstad - Showing me the truth

Mark Anastasi – For encouraging me to tell my story and write this book

# Bonus Material

Did you enjoy the book, but feel like you need more training? If you find somebody that has accomplished what you want to do, then I strongly suggest you model what they have done and train with them if you can. To help you on your way after reading *Never Work Again* I have a selection of resources that you can access for **FREE!**

Never Work Again is my second book. The first, entitled **Outsourcing Mastery: 17 Secrets for Outsourcing to the Philippines,** covers everything you need to know to outsource successfully to the Philippines – my favorite country for outsourced workers.

To grab your free copy just click the following link now: http://youwillneverworkagain.com/outsourcing_mastery/.

**FREE training videos** - http://www.worklessearnmore.tv

My FREE training videos shows you how to monetize your passion by applying automation and outsourcing in your business so you can live your freedom in 10 simple steps. The world's laptop millionaires, entrepreneurs and the 'New Rich' have all escaped the 9 to 5 using these exact strategies.

# HARDCORE

**Check out my podcast Hardcore MBA**
Go to www.hardcoremba.com

**Done-4-You Virtual Assistant Training Online (FREE),** go to http://www.mroutsourceuniversity.com/fe/43876-mr-outsource-university-free-training

At Mr Outsource University we provide an in-depth quality learning environment for people like you who want to experience Virtual Assistant training and performance mastery at its best.

Outsourcing to the Philippines, Done-4-You! Our recruitment service can find you **"The One",** your first outsourced employee! 30% OFF Mr.Outsource.com recruitment services. Use the code YWNWA in the subject area and we will find the perfect employee for you in the Philippines.

**The Freedom Boot Camp** - http://thefreedombootcamp.com/

With this proven system, I will show you that anyone with the drive and ambition to be successful can live like I do today – working only a few hours a week, and making up to $20,000 a month. It sounds impossible, if you have the mindset of a worker – but we're gonna teach you how to spin that around, and have the mindset of an entrepreneur.

**In The Freedom Bootcamp, you will learn:**

- How to switch from thinking like a worker, to thinking like an entrepreneur

- How to start a no-money down business that can make you up to $20,000 every month

- How to leverage other people's time to work only twenty hours a month

- How to automate your business, so you hardly even need to think about it

- How to create a lifestyle that lets you live out your dreams

- All with just a few easy-to-implement tools and tricks

One on One coaching with Erlend Bakke is possible if you are the right match. Erlend only works with entrepreneurs and business owners that are committed to their success and to living a life of freedom. Prices start at $10,000.

If you think this might be for you, please email erlend@mroutsource.com

# Your Free Copy of Outsourcing Mastery

**To grab your free copy of my first book, Outsourcing Mastery**, just click:
http://youwillneverworkagain.com/outsourcing_mastery.

*Outsourcing Mastery: 17 Secrets for Outsourcing to the Philippines* covers everything you need to know to outsource successfully to my favorite country for workers. *Outsourcing Mastery* tells you what you need to know whether you want just a single Virtual Assistant or whether you're planning on having a whole team of outsourcers! There's a lot of material that I didn't have space for in this book, so to make sure you have all the information you need, I'm simply going to give you a free copy of Outsourcing Mastery as my gift to you.

**Your free copy is available at**
http://youwillneverworkagain.com/outsourcing_mastery.

# 3Sixty Learn

Thanks once again for buying this book – but this time, the thanks aren't just from me. They're also from the people who benefit from the **3Sixty Learn program**, which helps train Filipinos from unfortunate backgrounds to use computers and to make a living working online. Throughout the book I emphasize the need to treat outsourced Filipino workers well, and to give value back to society in general – and I try my best to 'walk the talk'. To that end, **10% of my royalties from sales of this book will be donated to the program** to help keep this work going.

# About the Author

**Erlend Bakke** is a Norwegian serial entrepreneur, speaker, and #1 international bestselling author born in 1981 in London, UK. He currently owns the following three companies: *Mr. Outsource*, *3sixty*, and *3sixtyfactory*. Erlend speaks on the topics of entrepreneurship with focus on how to automate and outsource your business to avoid the trap of becoming a business prisoner. He spends most of his time between London, Oslo, and Davao City in the Philippines, but is available to speak at venues all over the world depending on availability.

Erlend trains entrepreneurs in how to start, run, and own freedom businesses through his seminar `The Freedom Bootcamp` (www.thefreedombootcamp.com), the membership website www.worklessearnmore.tv, and his weekly business podcast `Hardcore MBA Podcast` (www.hardcoremba.com). In 2013 he first published the book **Never Work Again** that went on to become an *#1 International Bestseller*. The book is focused on applying freedom to your life as well as your business by cutting the crap and getting real about your true needs and desires.

**You can email Erlend at: erlend@mroutsource.com**

**YouWillNeverWorkAgain.com/bonus**

## ALSO BY
# ERLEND BAKKE & STEVE SHOULDER

erlendbakke.com  Erlend Bakke Publishing

29925088R00140

Printed in Great Britain
by Amazon